BEGIN AGAIN

Neil Freebern

Copyright © 2026 by Soundwork Productions

All rights reserved. No part of this book may be reproduced or used in any manner without the prior written permission of the copyright owner, except for the use of brief quotations in a book review.

Disclaimer: The information contained in this book is for educational and inspirational purposes only and reflects the author's personal experiences with hearing loss, career transition, and mindfulness. It is not intended as a substitute for professional medical advice, diagnosis, or treatment. The author is not a medical doctor, audiologist, or licensed therapist. Always seek the advice of your physician or other qualified health provider with any questions you may have regarding a medical condition, tinnitus, or mental health concerns.

Cover design: Neil Freebern

"Upekkhā" lyrics © Neil Freebern — Soundwork Productions

First Edition: 2026

ISBN: 979-8-9942645-0-8 (Paperback)

ISBN: 979-8-9942645-1-5 (E-book)

PRELUDE

The Fracture

At some point, life stops unfolding the way we expected.

A role no longer fits. A body changes. A relationship shifts. A future we trusted begins to blur. Sometimes the break is sudden. Sometimes it gathers quietly, loss by loss, strain by strain, until one day we realize we are no longer standing in the life we thought we knew.

When that happens, most of us respond in familiar ways. We try to understand. We try to repair. We look for a path back to what felt stable. We tell ourselves that if we can just make sense of what happened, perhaps we can regain our footing. This book begins there, not with a solution, but with a disruption.

For most of my life, I found meaning in music. I taught it, conducted it, produced it, and performed it. My days were shaped by rehearsal, refinement, and the discipline of listening closely in the pursuit of shaping sound. Music was not simply my profession. It was the structure around which I understood my life. Then, one day in early spring, I damaged my left ear.

The change was instant. Everything I heard was distorted, buried beneath a layer of static that masked the beauty sound had once carried. My acoustic world had been reduced to the crackle of a song struggling to be heard through an old, poorly tuned AM radio.

My most trusted sense had been injured, and sound itself had become intolerable and painful. Within days, my hearing deteriorated further, and with it came tinnitus, a constant swirling ring inside my ear.

Silence was gone.

My losses became apparent almost immediately. I could not play my horn, conduct my ensembles, or continue my production work in the studio without extreme discomfort. A life I had spent decades building changed almost overnight. I was left in uncertainty, with the ringing in my ear marking every quiet moment like proof, that the life I had known could not simply resume.

But what followed inside me mentally was even more disorienting than the injury itself. Before I had fully absorbed what had occurred, my mind had already reached for a verdict.

This is ruin.
This is permanent.
This is the end of the life I knew.

At the time, those thoughts did not feel like interpretations. They felt like truth—I am broken.

That distinction matters more than I understood then. The deeper disturbance was not only the loss itself, but how quickly my mind took a painful event and began turning it into meaning. What happened to my hearing was real, but almost immediately, my mind began shaping that reality into a larger conclusion about who I was, what my future would be, and what my life now meant.

What I did not yet understand was that this reckoning had not begun with my ear alone. The injury landed on ground that had already been weakening for some time. Loss had been gathering quietly for years. Grief. Strain. Disillusionment. The slow erosion of roles and certainties I had trusted. By the time my hearing was compromised, something in me was already standing on unsteady ground.

Still, the question that stayed with me was not only what had occurred. It was what my mind kept doing as it tried to make sense of it all. That question became the doorway to everything that followed.

This is not a memoir about hearing loss, though hearing loss opened the door. It is not a story about bouncing back, and it is not an argument for optimism. It is an inquiry into what happens inside us when life rearranges itself without our permission, and how quickly the mind begins making meaning from the wreckage.

We do not simply live through what happens. We interpret it. We attach meaning to it. When pain is fresh, that meaning can harden quickly into a story about who we are, what life is, and what we should expect from the world.

Over time, I began to notice something unsettling. Emotional pain was one thing. The mind's relationship to that pain was another.

There was the raw fact of loss, and then there was the story being built around it. The body registered the experience, and the mind moved quickly to name it, explain it, and defend its explanation. It reached backward for evidence and forward into fear. It built a version of reality that felt complete, even when it was being assembled from memory, conditioning, and old conclusions I had never fully examined.

That discovery did not remove grief. It did not restore my hearing. It did not spare me the confusion of losing a life I had trusted. It created enough space to pause, to notice, and to question what had once felt absolute.

Inside that small space, my attention began to change. I became less focused on the loss itself and more curious about what my mind did in the aftermath. How quickly it reached for meaning. How eagerly it gathered evidence. How convincingly it turned pain into a story about my life.

That shift became the center of this book.

I began to study the reaction itself, not only the thoughts that came afterward, but the first stirrings beneath them: the tightening in my chest, the drop in my stomach, the surge that arrived before explanation. I began to sense that my mind was not meeting each moment from neutral ground. It was meeting life through a lens shaped by memory, fear, longing, habit, and the old patterns through which I had learned to understand myself.

Before long, I could see that what I called reality was often something more complicated. It was the moment itself, yes, but also the body's reaction to it, the mind's interpretation of it, and the story that formed around it. That realization was humbling.

I was not simply living through pain. I was living inside the meanings my mind had constructed around pain. The mind was trying to protect me, to explain the rupture, to create order from uncertainty. But in doing so, it often narrowed the world around the wound.

This book grew from that realization. Not from the injury alone, but from the question that followed it: What happens inside us when the mind turns pain into a story, and then teaches us to live as if the story is the whole truth?

I can only explore these questions through the events of my own life, but the patterns I began to see were not mine alone. They were human patterns: the way we react to loss, the way we reach for meaning, the way the mind turns pain into identity, and the way we slowly learn to see again.

You do not need to have lost your hearing to recognize this terrain. You only need to know what it is to have life interrupt your plans, to feel the ground shift beneath a future you thought you understood, and then be asked, somehow, to keep living without the map that once made sense.

If you are reading this from inside your own season of fracture, I am not here to minimize what hurts or rush you toward some polished lesson. What has happened to you, matters. Loss matters. Grief matters. The body knows when something real has been taken, and there is no wisdom in pretending otherwise. But there may come a moment, as there did for me, when another question quietly rises beneath the first one. Not only, why did this happen? But also, what is happening in me as I meet it?

That question changed the direction of my life.

It did not offer immediate relief. It offered something quieter and, in time, more useful: curiosity, attention, and a different way of standing inside the same experience.

That is what these pages are really about. They are about disruption, yes, but also about perception. About the body, the mind, identity, emotion, and the stories we inherit and continue to tell ourselves. About the possibility that awareness can interrupt what once felt automatic. About what falls apart, and what begins to emerge when we stop assuming our first interpretation is the whole truth.

If your life has ever changed in ways you did not choose, then some of what follows may feel familiar. This is where it begins.

CHAPTER ONE

Taking It Apart

When my hearing injury arrived and my life seemed to grind to a halt, my reaction was hardly surprising. I was devastated. I began grieving in a way I had never known before. Not sadness. Not ordinary mourning. Something heavier, as if the floor beneath me had given out and I was falling through space with nothing solid to grab onto.

Only later would I find language for that kind of collapse. St. John of the Cross in the 16th century called it the *dark night of the soul*, a profound. darkness that does not simply make life painful but takes apart the very meanings that once held a life together.

At the time, I had no such language. I only knew that everything felt as if it were breaking at once. The life I had built around music no longer felt intact. The roles I had depended on were slipping away, and I had no idea what, if anything, might take their place.

In those early weeks, I wrote constantly to make sense of my new reality.

At first, I was not writing to understand anything. I was writing to survive the force of what I was feeling. I was trying to shape the pain into language, to make it visible, maybe even beautiful enough that someone else might understand it, even provide me empathy. Some part of me wanted the writing to prove the depth of my loss. I wanted the page to confirm that what I was living through was real, devastating, and worthy of grief.

One of those early passages read like this:

> "That night, as I left the music hall, my gut felt heavy, and my thoughts scattered like static. I sat in my car, alone in the dark parking lot, hands resting on the wheel, unable to move. My world had just split in two, the before and the after. The streetlight outside cast a pale circle across the dashboard while the swirling harmonics of my tinnitus stole the silence..."

When I read that months later, I try not to judge it. It was honest. It captured something true about the shock of it all. But I can also see that something else was happening beneath the writing. I wanted the language to hold me in my brokenness. I wanted the story to validate the magnitude of what had happened. The more I wrote from inside that identity, the more solid it became. The more it defined me as broken.

Each retelling reinforced the same conclusion. This is final. This defines me. Nothing meaningful can exist beyond this loss. I did not realize it at the time, but I was not only describing my suffering. I was deepening it. Still, something in me kept returning to the page.

At some point, the writing began to shift. I started to wonder whether what I was living through might look different from another angle. Early in my reckoning, I came across a parable that opened that possibility.

> **The Old Man Lost His Horse**
>
> A poor farmer once lost his only horse.
> His neighbors said, "How unfortunate."
> The farmer replied, "Maybe so, maybe not."
>
> The next day, the horse returned with three wild horses. "How wonderful," said the neighbors.
> Again, the farmer replied, "Maybe so, maybe not."
>
> When his son later broke his leg trying to ride one of them, they said, "How terrible."
> The farmer said, "Maybe so, maybe not."
>
> Soon after, soldiers came through the village to conscript young men. Seeing the boy's broken leg, they passed him by. The neighbors said, "How fortunate."
>
> The farmer replied, "Maybe so, maybe not."

The story did not relieve my pain. My hearing was not improving. My work was not returning. Nothing external had changed in any reassuring way. Yet something in me had begun to shift. Slowly, almost without realizing it, I became less interested in the story of my loss and more interested in how my mind was retelling it.

The parable did not comfort me. It unsettled me. It suggested there might be another way to see what had happened, or at least another way to meet it. For the first time, I began watching what my mind was doing with my pain instead of simply declaring my life ruined.

The pain remained. But my curiosity, which had always been part of me, began pointing in a different direction. I was no longer only asking, how do I fix this? I was beginning to ask, how is my mind turning this pain into a story about my entire life?

In some ways, that instinct had been in me for a long time.

When I was young, I watched my brother rebuild the engine of his old Opel GT. The garage floor would be covered in parts, every bolt and gasket laid out carefully. He had a way of approaching broken things that stayed with me. He did not simply stand there cursing the engine and demanding that it work. He opened it up. He studied it. He traced the sequence, looking for the point where one thing affected another.

Sometimes he got frustrated, but he always returned to the question beneath the frustration.

How does this actually work?

Without fully realizing it, that is what I had begun doing with my own mind. I was laying the pieces of my suffering across the floor, not because I wanted to reduce it to parts, but because I could no longer live inside it without understanding how it was being assembled.

Through my writing, I started noticing patterns. A sensation would arise in my body, a tightening in my chest, a drop in my stomach, heat behind my eyes. Almost instantly, a thought would attach itself.

This is permanent.
You are finished.
This proves something about your worth.

The thought would trigger more sensation. The sensation would seem to confirm the thought. Back and forth it went, building momentum.

I began to see that the injury was real, but the suffering I was experiencing had layers. Some of those layers came from the injury itself. Others were being constructed in real time by the meanings my mind was attaching to it. That realization did not erase the grief or soften the loss. But it created the faintest bit of space. At that point, even that was enough.

I remember one afternoon in early spring, sitting outside with a warm cup of coffee beside me. I was very low that day, deep in the heaviness of all that had happened. My hearing was altered. My future still felt uncertain. Nothing about the larger reality of my life had resolved itself. I had begun writing about my experience, hoping the words might offer some kind of relief, when a spring breeze moved across my shoulders and caused me to pause.

I looked up from the page.

Then an old phrase rose in me, one I had learned as a boy at camp.

Stop and think.

It was simple. Almost too simple. But in that moment, it arrived like an instruction from some older, quieter part of my life.

So, I stopped.

The pasture stretched out in front of me, framed by the mountains beyond it. New growth was beginning to creep up the hillside. Birds moved through the air, singing into the morning. Cows grazed near the river. My dog came over and settled at my feet.

I took a breath.

For the first time in days, maybe weeks, I realized something I had not been able to feel. In this very moment, I was actually okay.

Not my life. Not the future. Not the grief. I did not mean that everything was fine, or that the loss had softened, or that I had found some hidden lesson. I meant something smaller. More immediate. More unsettling.

This moment was still here.
Somehow, so was I.
This moment was livable

It was as if, for one brief second, I woke up inside the storm of my own mind. The injury was still real. The grief was still real. Nothing had been solved. But I could suddenly see that my thoughts had become a weather system of their own, moving across everything in front of me. They had covered the beauty of the pasture, the coffee, the warmth of the sun, the breath in my body.

Life was still there. I had only been looking at it through the storm.

My circumstances were still painful and unresolved. Nothing had been fixed. Nothing had been restored. But for the first time, I could feel a distinction. The grief, the fear, the imagined future, the memory of what had been lost, all of it was active in me, and all of it mattered. But none of it was the same as the sunlight on my skin. None of it was the same as the air touching my face, the beauty of the mountains in front of me, or the breath moving through my body.

That was the first crack in the spell. Life had not disappeared. My perception of it had.

That realization did not end the grief or quiet the ringing in my ear, but it opened a small space inside the experience. A place where I could begin to see that the mind was not only witnessing my pain, but it was also carrying it forward, replaying it, projecting it, and laying it over the life still happening in front of me. When the narrative in my head paused, even for a breath, my experience changed with it.

That was not healing. It was observation. Observation became the beginning of a different kind of attention, a different form of awareness.

In the weeks that followed, I kept returning to that question. If the present moment itself was not always the source of my suffering, then what was? If grief could still be present while the sun warmed my skin, if loss could still be real while the field continued in front of me, then something important was happening inside my own perception.

My mind was not simply reporting the pain. It was gathering it, replaying it, projecting it forward, and spreading it across the whole of life. That realization changed the question. I was no longer asking only, how do I survive what happened? I was beginning to ask something deeper.

What is my mind doing with what happened?

I did not yet have a framework for any of this. I only had curiosity, and even that was fragile. But curiosity was enough to begin changing the way I wrote. The page stopped being only a place to describe my devastation. It became a place to track the movement of my mind.

I began reading more widely. Psychology. Philosophy. Contemplative practice. Not because I was trying to assemble a system, but because I could sense that something in me was beginning to watch rather than simply drown. If there was a mechanism beneath my reactions, I wanted to see it more honestly.

So, I started bringing my attention to what was happening in real time. Sensations. Thoughts. Emotions. The room around me.

I tried to notice experience as it unfolded instead of being pulled immediately into reaction. When I did get pulled, which was often, I wrote about that too. I studied the chain. How quickly a sensation became an emotion. How quickly that emotion became a story. How convincingly the story reshaped my sense of self. The shift was subtle, but it changed the direction of everything that followed.

My loss was real. The pain was real. But the meaning I was attaching to it was not simply arriving from the outside world. I was participating in its construction. That realization did not comfort me. It unsettled me.

It meant I could no longer place all of my suffering outside myself. It meant the mind had a role in shaping what I was living through. But it also meant that paying attention mattered. If interpretation was involved, then inquiry was possible. If inquiry was possible, then perhaps I was not as trapped inside the first story my mind told me as I had assumed. That was the quiet pivot.

My writing no longer needed to prove how broken I was. It began asking a different question:

How do we interpret what happens to us, and how do those interpretations quietly shape our suffering?

That question became the real beginning of this journey. Not because I had found an answer, but because I had started looking differently. Curiosity was beginning to take the place of collapse.

If your life has ever shifted in ways you did not choose, then some of this terrain may feel familiar. If you have ever felt defined by a moment that seemed final, you may understand why I began examining my reactions instead of only my loss.

I did not begin with clarity. I began by paying attention.

To the noise in my mind.
To the tension in my body.
To the stories I was telling myself about what my life had become.

What began as observation slowly became the first step toward understanding.

Chapter Two

The Mind's Reflex

When my life appeared to be falling apart, I kept reaching for something, anything, that could help me make sense of the wreckage. I wasn't searching for inspiration. I was searching for footing.

Somewhere in that fog, I found myself back inside the words of Viktor Frankl. He had endured levels of suffering most of us cannot imagine, yet what struck me was not his endurance. It was his insistence that even in the most brutal conditions, something remained intact.

Not comfort. Not control. But the capacity to choose how to respond.

Frankl wrote about meaning, but he did not treat it as an abstract idea. For him, meaning lived in small decisions. In how a person carried himself. In how he spoke to another. In the stance he took toward circumstances he could not change.

The line that lodged itself in me was simple and exact. In *Man's Search for Meaning*, he writes: Even when we have no control over our circumstances, we still retain one freedom—the freedom to choose how we respond to what happens.

I kept circling that sentence. **The freedom to choose how we respond to what happens.**

At first, I could not feel that freedom at all. When my hearing collapsed, choice felt fictional. The only option I could imagine was repair. Fix it. Reverse it. Undo it. I chased appointments, researched possibilities, searched for the right specialist, the right intervention, the right answer. My attention stayed locked on the circumstance itself, as if the right solution could restore the life I recognized.

But Frankl was not talking about changing the event. He was pointing toward the stance taken inside the event.

The longer I obsessed over why my life had shattered, the more I realized I was working on the wrong problem. My hearing might not be fixable. The past was certainly not reversible. But how I was meeting the moment, that was still unfolding in real time. That was the only place choice actually lived.

To reclaim that agency, I had to stop arguing with the outcome and start studying how I was meeting it. I wanted to get beneath the story my mind was producing about what had happened.

Many approaches to changing how we feel begin by asking us to work directly with our thoughts. Notice the thought. Question it. Replace it with one that leads somewhere better. I understand the value in that, and I do not dismiss it. But I found that by the time a thought was fully visible to me, much had already happened. My body had reacted. The moment had already been sorted. Meaning was already beginning to form. I was not choosing from neutral ground. I was stepping into a process already underway.

That was what made me want to look more closely at the reflex itself. I was not only interested in learning how to think differently. I wanted to understand why certain thoughts arrived with such force in the first place. I wanted to see how sensation became meaning, how meaning became story, and how story gathered enough momentum to feel like truth.

The goal, for me, was still the same. I wanted to respond with more freedom and less reactivity. But I could see that if I waited until the thought had fully formed, I was already late in the sequence. Something in me had already tightened. Something had already leaned toward fear, or away from discomfort, or begun searching for proof. The mind was not inventing its story from nowhere. It was organizing a reaction already in motion.

That is why this inquiry begins earlier. Not with the finished thought, but with the machinery that gives rise to it. Not only with what I was thinking, but with how the moment landed, how the body responded, how meaning started forming, and how a passing experience could harden into suffering before I even understood what was happening. Only then did a different response begin to feel possible.

As I paid closer attention to this process, a pattern began to emerge. The details of my days kept changing, but the internal response was strangely familiar. In charged moments, something in me would slip into autopilot, scanning for relief and quietly deciding what the moment meant.

What I was seeing was not careful thought. It was reflex.

Something happens. The body reacts. The mind interprets. A story forms. The mind begins looking for evidence that the story is true. Then the whole thing feeds back into itself. That is what I mean by the mind's reflex.

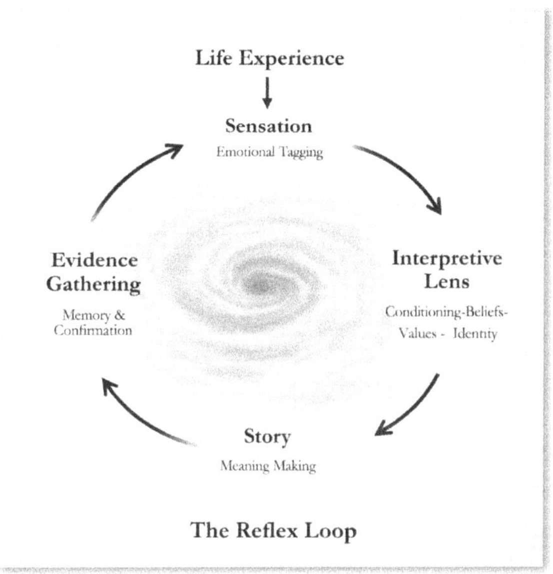

Experience begins with the senses. Something happens, and the nervous system registers it as sensation, a tightening in the chest, a drop in the stomach, heat behind the eyes, a rush of energy through the body.

Most of the time, sensation is simply information. The moment passes through us and fades. But when the signal carries enough emotional charge, it does not pass through cleanly. The body reacts first. Before a sentence has fully formed, the system has already flagged the moment as important, threatening, painful, or destabilizing.

Then the mind moves in to explain what the body is feeling. It tags the raw signal as emotion: fear, grief, anger, shame. Very quickly, that emotion starts shaping identity.

"I feel afraid" becomes "I am afraid."
"I feel broken" becomes "I am broken."

That shift matters. The emotion is no longer just something moving through experience. It begins attaching itself to the self. From there, the mind measures the moment against the life you thought you were living.

Does this fit who I am?
Does this threaten what I rely on?
Does this confirm something I already fear?

If the experience aligns with your expectations, the system settles. If it does not, the reflex moves to its next task. The mind begins building a story to restore coherence. It explains what happened. It predicts what comes next. It organizes the emotional charge into something that feels intelligible.

Once that story begins to take shape, the mind does something even more convincing. It starts gathering evidence.

This is the stage that can feel the most rational, because it no longer seems emotional. It feels like you are simply thinking it through. Looking at the facts. Being honest about reality. But in a charged state, evidence is rarely neutral.

The nervous system is already braced, and the mind begins selecting details that match the brace. It highlights what confirms the story and overlooks what complicates it. The body tightens, and that tightening gets treated as proof. The surge itself begins to feel like information. That is why reflex is so difficult to see while it is happening.

You do not feel like you are spiraling.
You feel like you are figuring it out.

When my own mind searched for meaning after the injury, it did not look back for medical explanations. It looked back for confirmation that I was broken.

My losses began to gather into a single story, as if everything were conspiring to confirm that my life had been marked by suffering. The loss of my sister. The passing of a beloved student. Personal health concerns. The dismantling of my music program after the pandemic and the unraveling of my teaching career. Then— the damage to my hearing. Experiences that had once belonged to separate chapters of my life were now being assembled into a single argument.

At first, it felt like memory. But the more closely I watched it, the more I could see that memory was being arranged like evidence in a trial. My mind was not revisiting these experiences randomly. It was building a case. The verdict was already taking shape.

I came to think of this as emotional stacking. Like a lawyer building an argument, the mind pulls forward every emotionally charged event that supports the conclusion it has already begun to reach. Separate losses start to gather under one narrative. Each one brings its own weight, and together they seem to prove what the body already fears.

In my case, the conclusion was simple and devastating. I was broken.

Once that verdict took hold, my mind no longer moved through time cleanly. It began oscillating between the past and the future. It looked backward for evidence that I had always been broken, then lurched forward into imagined futures shaped by that same conclusion. In the process, the present became harder and harder to inhabit.

If my hearing is damaged, then I can't play music.
If I can't play music with others, then I lose my community.
If I lose my community, then I lose my friends.
If I lose my friends, then I am alone.
If I am alone, then I am broken in every way.

That is how reflex deepens suffering. The mind gathers from the past, then projects into the future, and each projection stirs the body again. My chest tightened. My stomach dropped. My heart began to race all over again.

My mind took that renewed surge of sensation as proof, but the deeper issue was that the sensation itself kept the reflex alive. The story stirred the body, the body generated fresh sensation, and that sensation demanded interpretation all over again. The original event was over, yet the reflex kept reactivating because the body would not stop feeding it. By then, I was no longer responding freely to what had happened. I was living inside the reflex, increasingly confined by the interpretation I had built around it.

Once I saw that clearly in my own suffering, I began noticing that the same mechanism was not limited to major ruptures. It was woven into ordinary human experience. In fact, one of the clearest places to watch it at work is often at night when you toss and turn in bed trying to sleep.

Nothing is happening. The room is quiet. The day is over. Yet the inner system keeps running. You lie there staring at the ceiling while the mind turns the same material over and over, as if one more pass through the problem might finally deliver relief.

We have all been there. A conversation gets replayed. A look gets reinterpreted. A possibility gets expanded into a future. The body joins in immediately. A thought lands and the chest tightens. A memory surfaces and the stomach drops. What feels like analysis is also reactivation.

The mind believes it is working the problem, but each pass through the story stirs the body again, and the body's reaction gives the story more authority. The result is a closed loop: interpretation activates sensation, and sensation reinforces interpretation.

Neuroscientists often describe something like this through predictive processing. The mind makes a quick guess about what the feeling means, then looks for signals that confirm the guess. The body reacts, and the reaction seems to validate the interpretation.

You are no longer simply thinking about the experience.
You are inhabiting the body's verdict.

The mind wants relief. It believes the right explanation will settle the system. So, it keeps turning the problem like a Rubik's cube, certain that one more move will solve it.

Sometimes sleep comes not because anything has been resolved, but because exhaustion interrupts the loop. The charge does not disappear. It settles beneath awareness, waiting for the next moment that resembles the last one closely enough to call it back.

That was one of the most important realizations for me.

My suffering was not unfolding at random. It was following a sequence. Once I could see that sequence in moments of discomfort, I began noticing its structure elsewhere too. What surprised me was how familiar that structure felt.

Years earlier, I worked closely with a colleague who introduced me to design thinking. He described it as a disciplined way of approaching complex problems: define the real issue, gather context, test possibilities, verify what fits, refine the response. As we began bringing that framework into our teaching, we created a simple acronym for students:

DRIVE
Define. Research. Iterate. Verify. Evaluate.

At the time, this way of thinking belonged to classrooms, rehearsals, and creative work. I never imagined it had anything to do with suffering. That recognition came later.

As I began tracing the reflex in my own life, I realized the architecture felt familiar. The mind was moving through a kind of rapid, unconscious design process. Something happened. Sensation rose. Meaning was assigned. The mind searched memory, drafted an explanation, verified it against bodily and emotional evidence, and settled into a conclusion that felt coherent enough to believe.

The structure was similar. The difference was speed.

Design thinking is deliberate. It relies on pause, reflection, and revision. The mind's reflex runs a parallel kind of sequence almost instantly, without awareness. It interprets, verifies, and concludes before we realize it is happening.

That realization did not relieve my grief, but it clarified the mechanism. I was not simply having thoughts. I was constructing meaning. I was taking raw sensation and turning it into a narrative I could live inside.

My suffering no longer felt like a shapeless storm. I could feel the structure underneath it, and that structure can be observed. The reflex was fast, convincing, and largely invisible to me until I slowed down enough to watch it. Once I stopped arguing with the event itself, I began tracing the reflex that turned pain into suffering.

What can be observed can sometimes be interrupted. If I wanted to understand the reflex more honestly, I had to begin at its earliest point, before the full story took over, before interpretation hardened into certainty.

I had to begin with the first sensation that appears in the body.

Chapter Three

How Experience Enters the Body

Most of us move through life assuming our emotional reactions are simply caused by what happens around us. Something hurts, so we feel hurt. Someone says something sharp, so anger rises. The feeling seems to confirm the moment. It feels obvious, almost self-explanatory.

But over time, I began to notice something more unsettling. My reaction often appeared before I had fully understood what had happened.

A tone of voice could tighten something in me before I had consciously interpreted the words. A small comment could stir discomfort before I had decided whether it was kind, dismissive, or threatening. The body seemed to register the moment first, while the mind hurried in afterward to explain it. If I wanted to interrupt the reflex, I had to begin where it actually begins, in the body.

Every moment of life reaches us through the senses. Light becomes sight. Vibration becomes sound. Pressure becomes touch. Temperature, posture, movement, scent, expression, all of it arrives as raw information moving through the body. Within fractions of a second, the nervous system begins sorting that information. Most of it passes quietly. But some signals stand out. Something in us registers them as significant before we know what they mean.

That first registration is often subtle. A contraction. A quickening. A heaviness. A flicker of unease. A small lift toward something pleasant. Long before a full emotion takes shape, the body has already begun responding.

When that sensation appears, it does not remain undefined for long. Something in us quickly registers how strong it feels, how much it seems to matter, and the basic tone with which it lands. Pleasant. Unpleasant. Neutral. That early sorting happens fast, often before conscious thought catches up. It is one of the first steps in meaning-making, because it begins organizing the moment before the story has even formed.

This matters because it is also where desire and aversion begin. The body leans toward what feels pleasant. It recoils from what feels unpleasant. It barely marks what feels neutral. From that first leaning come the earliest seeds of liking and disliking, grasping and resistance, wanting more or wanting away. The mind will soon build a story around those movements, but the movements themselves begin earlier, in the body. They are part of what gives shape to the interpretive lens through which the moment will soon be understood.

In Buddhist psychology, there is a word for this first feeling tone of experience: **vedanā**. It refers to the immediate way a moment lands before the mind begins building a story around it. I did not need that word in order to feel the truth of it, but when I came across it, it named something I had already begun to notice. Experience arrives, and the body leans toward it, away from it, or barely registers it at all.

One late August morning, I woke with a heaviness I could not name. The dogs barked. The coffee steamed like any other day. Nothing dramatic had happened. Yet something in me felt low, dimmed somehow, as if a quiet fog had settled into my chest.

The feeling stayed with me, and for hours I tried to explain it away. Was I tired? Irritable? Just off for no reason? Every explanation felt thin. By the middle of the day, even small things began to bother me. The world had not changed much, but the way I was receiving it had. Only later did I understand what I was feeling. My family was preparing for the school year ahead, and I was not. For the first time in decades, I was not returning to a classroom.

My body knew first.
The story arrived later.

At the time, I had no language for that. I only knew that something in me had already reacted before thought could explain why. Later, Stephen Porges's language of **neuroception** helped me understand this a little more clearly. The nervous system is always scanning beneath awareness, registering cues of safety or threat before the thinking mind has caught up. My body was not betraying me. It was responding before I had words.

Still, that first signal is not yet the full story. It is not even always a clear emotion. Often it is just a bodily sense that something meaningful is here, even if the meaning has not yet taken form.

That is where philosopher and psychotherapist Eugene Gendlin's phrase **felt sense** became useful to me. He used it to describe that murky bodily knowing that appears before thought has fully organized experience into language. When I first encountered the term, I recognized it immediately. It was that morning heaviness I could not explain. That pressure in the chest before the thought appeared. That sense that something in me already knew, even when my mind had not caught up.

What gave Gendlin's work real force for me was that he was not only naming an inner phenomenon. He was pointing toward a way of meeting it. Instead of forcing an explanation, he suggests something quieter and more exacting. Pause. Turn inward. Stay with the bodily sense long enough for its shape to become clearer. Let the body offer a word, an image, or a quality that fits what is there. Then wait and see whether that fit is true.

When it is, something often shifts. The breath deepens. The chest softens. A little space opens. Gendlin called this a **felt shift**. Not because the problem has been solved, but because something real has been contacted before the mind had a chance to overtake it.

His work helped me make an important distinction. Vedanā is the first feeling tone with which experience lands. Felt sense is what becomes available when I stay with that first tone long enough for the body to reveal more of what it knows. One is immediate. The other deepens through attention.

That distinction mattered because if I moved too quickly, I skipped over both. The mind rushed in, named the moment, and turned it into a story before I had actually listened to what the body was telling me. But if I slowed down, even slightly, something else became possible. I could notice the signal before the narration took over.

This is what I began practicing in very simple ways. Instead of saying, "I am anxious," I started trying to notice what was actually happening.

My chest is tight.
There is heat in my face.
Something in me is bracing.

That may sound like a small shift, but it changes the entire relationship. The moment I name sensation as sensation; a little space opens between me and the feeling. I am no longer fully merged with the interpretation. I am closer to experience itself.

That space does not remove pain. It does not calm the nervous system instantly. But it gives me a way to stay near what is true without being swallowed so quickly by what the mind wants to make of it. It taught me something humbling: the body does not move on the mind's timeline. I could understand something intellectually and still feel my chest tighten as if the old danger were present. Awareness, then, was not only a matter of noticing. It was also a matter of **how** I noticed. The body did not usually open under force. It opened when it felt safe enough to be met.

So, the practice became less about explanation and more about permission.

Can I stay with this for one breath longer?
Can I notice where it lives in the body?
Can I let it be sensation before I turn it into a conclusion?

This is where the work truly begins. Not with a better explanation, but with the willingness to feel what is already here. The body registers. It leans. The mind begins to organize around that leaning. The story comes later. And if I wanted to understand suffering more honestly, I had to learn to listen there first.

Chapter Four

How Stories Form

Not long after my hearing changed, I began noticing how quickly my mind moved to explain even the smallest discomfort. A text would arrive with a tone I couldn't quite read, and before I had fully taken in the words, something in my body had already shifted. A tightening. A heaviness. A slight internal drop. By the time I consciously asked myself what the message meant, part of me was already bracing.

That was what started to interest me.

The body reacts first, but suffering deepens when the mind rushes in to explain the feeling. I began noticing how quickly it happened. A tone would shift, a silence would linger, and almost instantly my mind stepped in. What did that mean? Had I done something wrong? Was distance forming where closeness used to be? The moment itself was often small, sometimes even ambiguous, yet the meaning my mind built around it could arrive with surprising force.

When something unsettles us, the moment rarely stays unexplained for long. A comment lands strangely. A conversation ends with a tone that lingers. A look passes across someone's face, and something in the body shifts before the mind has words for it. There is a tightening, a heaviness, a small internal flinch that says this matters. Almost immediately, the mind begins searching for an explanation that fits the feeling already moving through the body.

That search does not begin from neutral ground. It begins inside a system already shaped by memory, emotional residue, expectation, and the many quiet conclusions we carry about who we are and how life tends to go. Beneath the surface of thought lives a whole history of impressions about belonging, safety, worth, love, rejection, competence, and threat. We do not build the meaning of a moment from nothing. We build it from materials that have been collecting in us for years.

This is why the mind can move so quickly from sensation to meaning. What arrives first in the body as a reaction begins looking for a shape it recognizes.

The moment is no longer just what happened. It is already being compared, measured, and filtered against what has happened before. That filter is what I have come to think of as the **interpretive lens**.

The lens is not a single belief, and it is not always easy to see. It is the accumulated structure of prior experience. It is made of memory, emotional learning, family atmosphere, reward, disappointment, repetition, fear, longing, and all the subtle ways life has trained us to expect what certain moments mean. Over time, those impressions stop feeling like impressions and start feeling like reality. The lens does not simply help us see. It quietly decides what stands out.

That is why two people can live through the same moment and come away with entirely different meanings. One person hears feedback and feels invited into growth. Another hears the same words and feels exposed. One person experiences silence and feels spaciousness. Another feels abandoned by it. The present moment may be shared, but the meaning is not. Meaning is filtered, and that filter is rarely as current as we assume it is. What feels like a reaction to now is often a response to what now resembles.

A delayed reply can awaken an old fear of being left. A distant tone can stir an old memory of criticism. A small mistake can touch an old belief that love or approval must be earned. The present is real, but the meaning attached to it is often older than the moment itself. This was one of the most important things I began to see in myself. I thought I was reacting to what was happening in front of me. More often, I was reacting to what the moment touched in me. The current event was acting like a key. The lock had been there for years.

This begins much earlier than most of us realize. Before we had words for our experience, we were already learning from the environments around us. A softened face, a cold tone, a delayed comfort, a warm response. The body was taking all of it in long before the thinking mind could explain anything. Over time, those repeated experiences became impressions about how life works: how closeness is earned, how safety is lost, what happens when you disappoint, what happens when you need too much, what kind of person gets welcomed, what kind gets corrected.

Those lessons do not always arrive as sentences. Often they live more quietly, as posture, guardedness, self-monitoring, performance, withdrawal, or the instinct to be useful before being fully oneself. The body learns the pattern first, and the mind explains it later. That is why so many of our stories feel obvious. They do not feel like stories at all. They feel like truth. They have been rehearsed below the level of language for so long that when the mind finally names them, it sounds less like interpretation and more like recognition.

That recognition can take many forms. It may sound like "I am too much," or "I am not enough," or "people leave," or "love has conditions," or "mistakes cost something." We do not always think those exact words, but we often live from them. That is what makes the lens so powerful. It allows old templates to masquerade as present truth. The mind does not usually say, "This reminds me of something unresolved." It says, "This is what is happening." It speaks with the authority of immediacy, even when it is organizing the moment through inherited patterns.

The more I saw this, the more I understood that the story of a moment is never just about the moment. It is about the meeting between what is happening now and what has already been learned. That meeting point is where suffering often deepens.

When my hearing collapsed, the loss itself was painful. But the meanings that formed around it were not only about hearing. They were shaped by a much older structure in me. The event did not remain a circumstance for long. It became personal. I was no longer just someone experiencing loss. The mind quickly drafted a more total conclusion. I was broken. I was diminished. I was no longer the person I had been. The event fused with identity.

That fusion is one of the mind's most convincing moves. A feeling becomes a conclusion, a conclusion becomes a self, and a moment becomes a definition. Once the story hardens into identity, it becomes much harder to question, because the mind is no longer only defending an interpretation. It is defending the self it has built from that interpretation.

This helps explain why even painful stories can feel stabilizing. A familiar wound can feel safer than an unknown future. A known conclusion can feel safer than ambiguity. The mind often prefers a painful coherence to an open question. That preference matters, because the story is not always chosen because it is true. Often it is chosen because it is familiar.

Many of the stories we carry began as adaptations. They helped us move through circumstances we did not yet know how to understand. They helped us preserve connection, predict emotional weather, avoid pain, or maintain some kind of internal order.

That is why old interpretations can be so persistent. They are not only distortions. They were once strategies. Some still protect. Some now confine. Many do both.

The important thing is not to shame the story for existing. The important thing is to see it forming. The moment I can sense that a story is taking shape, rather than simply becoming the story, something begins to loosen. I am no longer fully inside the lens. I am starting, however slightly, to look at it.

That shift does not erase conditioning. It does not wipe the past clean or free me instantly from interpretation. But it introduces a little daylight, and daylight matters. Once the lens becomes visible, the story loses some of its authority. It may still be persuasive. It may still arrive with emotional force. But it is no longer the only reality in the room.

Instead of assuming the moment means exactly what the mind says it means, another possibility opens. Maybe this reaction is current. Maybe it is inherited. Maybe both are true. That question alone can change the whole field of experience, not because it removes pain, but because it interrupts certainty.

For me, that interruption was the beginning of a different kind of honesty. I could begin asking what in this moment belongs to now, and what belongs to the past. I could ask what this kind of feeling had meant to me before, and what old template might be trying to pass itself off as truth again.

Those questions did not give me instant freedom, but they did create the possibility of seeing my life with a little more humility, a little less certainty, and a little more willingness to admit that what feels most obvious may not be the whole story.

That, for me, is where meaning begins to soften. Not when the mind stops interpreting, but when I realize interpretation is happening. Then the story is no longer invisible. Then the lens begins to reveal itself.

Once a story takes shape, the mind does not simply believe it. It begins gathering evidence to make it feel true.

Chapter Five

The Evidence Stage

Once the story begins, the mind does not just believe it. It starts building a case for it.

It does not arrive at an interpretation and simply move on. It goes back. It replays the conversation, revisits the moment, reconsiders the tone, reopens the feeling in the body, and keeps turning the material over as though one more pass through it might finally settle the question. This is what I came to think of as being **LIT**, **lost in thought**. The mind is no longer simply observing experience. It is under the influence of the story it has begun to build.

For a long time, this stage confused me because it no longer felt emotional in the obvious sense. It felt thoughtful. It felt as if I were being honest with myself, carefully examining what had happened and trying to understand it. But beneath that surface, another process was unfolding. The mind was not simply remembering. It was trying to verify.

That is what gives the evidence stage its force. It does not feel like distortion. It feels like due diligence. The mind is asking questions.

Does this interpretation fit?
Is this really what this means?
Does this line up with what I already know about life, about other people, about myself?

The replay has a function. The system is searching for resonance.

After my hearing injury, I could spend hours moving through the same chain of thought. What happened. What it meant. What it would cost. What it revealed about me. Each return seemed to promise clarity, but the deeper effect was different. I was not getting closer to truth so much as strengthening a pattern. The story kept returning because the system was trying to determine whether it held.

To test it, my mind did something very predictable. It started comparing the story against the past.

Not for neutral information. Not for a balanced survey of memory. It looked for other moments that felt familiar, other experiences that carried a similar emotional shape. A loss. A humiliation. A separation. A disappointment. Something else that seemed to say the same thing the current story was already beginning to say.

This was the same process I earlier called emotional stacking, the mind pulling forward other charged experiences and laying them beside the current one as supporting evidence. Experiences that once belonged to separate chapters of life begin gathering under the same conclusion. The more familiar the emotional tone, the more persuasive the connection seems.

What makes emotional stacking so powerful is that those older experiences are not neutral memories. They still carry charge. Once they are recruited into the present story, that charge lands in the body again. The chest tightens. The stomach drops. The throat contracts. The body begins reacting not only to the current moment, but to the accumulated feeling of everything now being drawn into the same case.

That bodily reaction matters because the body does not just respond to the story. It feeds it.

The mind replays the interpretation. The interpretation recruits similar material. Those memories stir fresh sensation in the body. That sensation demands interpretation all over again.

This is the deeper mechanism of the evidence stage. The mind is not only confirming the story in thought. It is reactivating the body through emotionally charged memory, and the body's response gives the story more authority. The returning sensation feels like proof. It feels like confirmation that the interpretation must be right, because the body is now responding so strongly to it.

That is how the reflex keeps itself alive. Or, in the language that feels truest to me, that is what it means to be LIT.

The original event may be over, but the system is still feeding on the charge it continues to generate. The story activates the body. The body produces sensation. The sensation calls for explanation. The explanation strengthens the story. Then the whole thing circles back again.

This is why suffering can begin to feel self-confirming.

The mind says, *See? This hurts because it's true.* But what often goes unnoticed is that the pain is not coming only from the present interpretation. It is also coming from the old material that interpretation has awakened. The story is being tested against the past, and the past is answering through the body.

That is why this stage can feel so convincing. The body is really responding. The charge is real. The emotion is real. But the meaning attached to that charge is not neutral. It has already been shaped by the narrative that called the charge forward in the first place.

The longer I watched this process, the more I realized that being LIT was not merely a symptom of distress. It was the experiential form of the reflex itself. When the mind loops, compares, verifies, recruits the past, and reactivates the body, that is what being lost in thought actually is. The reflex is no longer just happening beneath awareness. It has become the atmosphere of consciousness. You are inside it, living in a mind that feels busy, concerned, analytical, and sincere, all while it keeps building support for the same conclusion.

That is why rumination can feel productive even while it is deepening pain. It is not random noise. It is the mind trying to make the story feel undeniable. Every time the body responds, the groove deepens. A thought returns. The body reacts. The reaction makes the thought feel more credible. The mind returns again.

Over time, the path becomes easier to travel. The story arrives faster. The body responds sooner. The whole system begins anticipating the conclusion before the evidence has even fully emerged. What once felt like a reaction starts becoming a default.

This is one of the ways our perceptions get trained.

The evidence stage is never only about the past. It is shaping the future. The more often a certain interpretation is rehearsed and confirmed, the more likely the system is to look for similar confirmation next time. The details that support the story become easier to see. The details that challenge it begin to fade. The narrative starts arriving preloaded.

That is how the mind begins narrowing the field of perception around what it already expects to be true.

This whole process does not remain internal. It often moves into speech. We tell the story.

We tell it to friends, to partners, to therapists, to ourselves in the car, in the shower, in bed at night. Sometimes that telling is necessary. Sometimes it is the beginning of healing. But retelling is not automatically release. Retelling can also serve the loop.

When a story is told and met only with more confirmation, more outrage, or more reinforcement of the same verdict, the charge can deepen. The body reenters the story. The interpretation grows more solid. The pain cycle continues.

But there is another possibility, one I only understood more fully later. A story can also be met with steadiness. With space. With a kind of listening that does not rush to prove the story true or false but helps us see it more clearly. I will return to that later, because it matters deeply. For now, what mattered most was simply recognizing that retelling could either reinforce the loop or begin to loosen it.

At that stage in my own reckoning, I mostly knew the kind of retelling that hardened the story. I was not only remembering what had happened. I was rehearsing what it meant.

Lately I have been noticing how tightly people grip their stories. You can hear it in conversation, the way the same framing returns, the same conclusion already waiting beneath the words. The details may change, but the underlying paradigm stays intact. At a certain point, the story is no longer helping a person understand experience. It is helping them preserve a self.

That kind of grip rarely forms all at once. It is built through repetition. Ancient teachers used the word **samskara** for these kinds of imprints, grooves left behind by repeated thought, feeling, and reaction. I find the image helpful. At first a path is barely visible. Then you walk it again. And again. Soon the grass begins to flatten. The next time you come to that patch of field, your feet move there almost automatically.

The mind works in much the same way.

Repetition gives the story authority. Add emotional charge, and that authority deepens. The story no longer returns as one interpretation among many. It returns with weight, familiarity, and the force of prior confirmation. It begins to feel less like a thought and more like reality.

This is where the courtroom image became useful to me.

By the time I noticed the process clearly, the roles were already in place. I was the prosecutor, gathering evidence for the story. I was the judge, deciding what the evidence meant. And I was the prisoner, living inside the verdict.

That was the deeper violence of this stage. The mind was no longer just reacting. It was building a system that could keep proving itself right. Memory supplied precedent. The body supplied sensation. Thought arranged both into argument. Imagination forecasted consequences. The case kept strengthening itself, not because reality had become clearer, but because the mind had become more committed to its own conclusion.

That is why suffering can begin to feel less like an experience and more like a sentence.

The mind interprets. It tests. It gathers support. It reactivates the body. Then it starts defending what it has built. By that point, the story is no longer just a passing explanation. It has started functioning like truth.

What changed for me was not that this process suddenly stopped. What changed was that I began recognizing it while it was happening. I could feel the shift from interpretation into advocacy. I could sense the moment when the mind stopped wondering and started proving. That recognition did not dissolve the loop, but it changed my relationship to it.

Instead of assuming that every repeated thought deserved my trust, I began asking a different question.

What is this repetition trying to prove?

That question opened something important. It revealed that the mind was not always circling because it was getting closer to truth. Sometimes it was circling because it was trying to secure a verdict it was not ready to release.

Once I could see that, another layer of the process became visible. Repetition was not only reinforcing the story. It was training perception, deepening the groove, and teaching the system how to see. Before long, the question was no longer just what the story proved.

It was what the story was beginning to say about who I was.

That is where the next stage begins.

Chapter Six

Identity's Grip

When the story hardens into identity, the moment stops being an experience and starts feeling like a definition of who I am. That is when identity tightens its grip.

A few years back, an impressive man moved to town from Los Angeles. He was an accomplished actor who loved to play saxophone on old jazz standards. Before long, we had put together a small combo and were meeting to play late into the evening.

I remember listening to him for the first time with a kind of admiration that went beyond technique. He had a raw, instinctive feel. Nothing about his playing sounded forced. He was not thinking his way through the tune. He was inside it. When he played one of his favorite standards, it felt as though he were stepping into something familiar and letting memory, instinct, and timing carry the phrase.

As I listened more closely, I noticed that when he landed on a note that did not belong to the changes, he did not flinch. You could hear the dissonance immediately. The harmony tightened, and for a split second the note hung there, exposed. But he did not retreat or apologize. He stayed with it. He turned the note, repeated it, shifted its placement, and worked it until what first sounded wrong became part of the line. The tension did not disappear. It transformed.

That is one of jazz's quiet lessons. A note is rarely wrong on its own. It becomes wrong when the musician freezes, hides from it, or rushes past it as though it must be erased. But when a player stays present, dissonance becomes material. It can open a new direction in the phrase. What first appears to be a mistake becomes an invitation.

Life often gives us the same opportunity. But that same evening, I learned how difficult that opportunity can be when identity is involved.

We started a new chart, and as the tune kicked off, I realized my lead sheet was in a different key. I had to transpose on the fly and, almost immediately, I was signaled to take a solo. My mind was still scrambling to find the new key center, and within seconds I was filling the room with notes that made very little musical sense.

Unlike the sax player, I did not stay with the dissonance. My body tightened. My attention narrowed. I stopped listening. The music kept moving, but I was no longer inside it. In an instant, the experience stopped being about sound and became about self.

That is the shift that matters.

A thing happened.
Then it began saying something about me.

The wrong notes did not remain wrong notes for long. They became evidence. Not just that I had missed the harmony, but that I was the kind of player who missed. Not just that I was uncomfortable, but that I did not belong inside the moment. The error became personal.

That is how identity enters the room.

It does not announce itself with philosophy. It appears in the speed with which an event becomes a statement about the self. Something happens, and almost immediately the mind converts it into meaning. Then that meaning hardens into implication.

I missed.
becomes
I am not good enough.

I felt exposed.
becomes
I do not belong here.

The situation changes, but the deeper injury comes from what the mind begins saying the situation means about who you are.

That night, I could feel the whole process unfolding in real time. My body constricted. My attention turned inward. I became LIT, under the influence of the story my mind was building. I was no longer hearing the music as music. I was hearing it through the verdict that was forming around me.

As the rehearsal continued, I was not called on to solo again. My mind seized on that immediately.

See? They know.

That was the moment the interpretation crossed over into identity. I was no longer responding to the tune, the room, or the actual shape of the evening. I was responding to what I believed the moment revealed about me. The solo ended, but the thought remained.

I suck.

What fascinates me now is not the mistake itself, but how quickly the mind turned it into a self. The music did not collapse. The room did not stop. No one threw down their instrument in disgust. Yet internally, something far more significant had already happened. I had begun building a version of myself inside that moment, and once that identity took shape, everything that followed started serving it.

Looking back, I can see how little actually happened on the surface. But on the inside, the event had touched something much older and more charged than a simple musical misfire. My reaction was not really about the notes. It was about what the wrong notes seemed to threaten.

This is where I found the work of Edward Deci and Richard Ryan unexpectedly helpful. Their Self-Determination Theory proposes that human beings tend to flourish when three core psychological needs are intact: **connection, competence, and agency**. When those supports are stable, we tend to stay open and responsive. When they are threatened, the system tightens.

That night, all three were touched at once.

Connection went first. The moment I faltered, I no longer felt in tune with the group. The experience was not just musical. It became relational. I felt separate, and separation carries a particular kind of charge. It strikes at our need to belong.

Then competence took the hit. My training had wired accuracy, preparedness, and fluency into my sense of safety. I trusted myself as a musician because I trusted my ability. The second that ability seemed compromised, the floor beneath me shifted. The mistake no longer felt like information. It felt like exposure.

Agency disappeared right after that. The moment I became self-conscious, I stopped inhabiting the music and started managing my image. Instead of responding from inside the experience, I was reacting to what I imagined it said about me. My attention was no longer free. It had been taken over by the need to recover, explain, or defend.

That is what identity-threat feels like from the inside. Not merely embarrassment, but contraction. The event becomes a threat to belonging, to competence, to your ability to remain steady inside yourself. Once those three begin collapsing at once, the mind does not calmly assess what happened. It moves to protection.

That is why identity is so easy to mistake for essence.

When the structure is threatened, the reaction feels immediate and personal. We assume we are protecting something permanent, something real and solid at the core. But the more closely I watched moments like that one, the more I began to suspect that what I was defending was not some fixed self, but a construction. A pattern. A story that had become familiar enough to feel like "me."

That suspicion deepened as I thought about the different identities I had lived inside over the years. Student. Teacher. Musician. Conductor. Composer. Each one felt substantial while I was inside it. Each one seemed to describe something stable and essential. But life kept moving, and those identities kept shifting with it.

Today, some of those roles are no longer active in my life, yet I can still feel how strongly the mind wants to defend them. The structure remains even when the circumstance has changed.

That revealed something important to me. Identity is not only made from what we do. It is made from the meanings we have attached to what we do, what it says about our worth, our place, our value, our right to belong.

That is why interpretation can become so powerful. A story does not stay a story for long. If it is rehearsed enough, defended enough, and reinforced enough, it begins functioning as selfhood.

The mind says, this happened.
Then, this means something.
Then, this says something about me.
Then, this is who I am.

That sequence is subtle, but it changes everything.

When my hearing was damaged and I had to step away from making music altogether, the loss struck every pillar my identity had been leaning on. My connection to the musical world changed. The competence I had spent decades building no longer felt trustworthy. My sense of agency weakened because the very instrument through which I had expressed myself no longer responded the way it once had.

The reflexive mind did what it knew how to do. It interpreted the loss, rehearsed it, and built a story around it. But underneath that story was something even more charged. The structure of self I had built around being a musician was under threat.

That was why the suffering felt so total.

The pain was not only in what had happened.
It was in what the event seemed to say about who I could no longer be.

The mind was not only grieving a change in circumstance. It was defending a self that had been organized around sound, ability, purpose, and belonging.

The event touched all of that at once. What I experienced as devastation was not simply the loss itself. It was the destabilization of the identity that had made the loss intelligible.

Once I could see that, something subtle but important shifted. I stopped treating identity as a fixed essence and began seeing it as a reactive structure under pressure. The self I was defending so fiercely was not false exactly, but neither was it solid in the way I had imagined. It was assembled from memory, role, habit, approval, repetition, and story. Life had helped shape it. So had fear. So had love. So had pain.

That realization did not erase my grief, but it did soften the panic around it. If identity is something shaped over time, then a threat to it does not mean I am being erased.

That did not mean the loss was small. It meant I no longer had to treat every threat to identity as proof that I was disappearing. I could begin to ask a different question.

What is actually being threatened here?

The answer was not always the self.
Often it was the structure the self had come to rely on.

That distinction matters, because once I could see identity as a structure rather than an essence, I could also see how quickly the mind moved to defend it. Perfectionism, control, withdrawal, people-pleasing, over-explaining, shrinking, performing, staying agreeable, avoiding risk, all of those can become ways the system tries to protect belonging, competence, and agency when identity feels unstable.

Seen this way, many of the traits we call personality are really forms of protection. They may look like character, but often they are defenses built around what the self has learned it must protect.

This is why identity has such a grip.

It does not only tell us who we are.
It tells us what must not be threatened.

Once that structure is in place, the mind starts organizing perception around its defense. The wrong note is no longer just a wrong note. The failed plan is no longer just inconvenience. The criticism is no longer just criticism. Everything begins leaning toward self-implication.

That is what makes identity so costly. It narrows the field. It makes experience personal even when it is partial, temporary, or ambiguous. It trains us to hear verdict where there may only be discomfort, to hear annihilation where there may only be change.

When I think back to that rehearsal, what stays with me is not the embarrassment of the solo. It is how quietly the rest of my future rearranged itself afterward. I turned down the next chance to play with the group. I pulled back. I let one charged moment define what I was willing to risk.

That is the cost of identity when it hardens around fear. It does not only explain the past. It starts editing the future.

What steadies me now is the memory of that sax player and the way he met dissonance. He did not abandon the note. He stayed with it long enough to hear what else it might become. I have come to think that this is not only a musical skill. It is a way of being with life.

If identity is a structure under pressure, then perhaps the work is not to defend it so fiercely. Perhaps the work is to stay with the moment long enough to see what it really is before turning it into a sentence about who I am.

That is not easy. The self tightens quickly. The old story comes fast. The mind becomes LIT and the atmosphere changes. But even there, something can begin to loosen. The event can remain difficult without becoming defining. The interpretation can arise without becoming identity. The structure can be seen without being mistaken for essence.

For me, that is where a different kind of freedom begins. Not in shedding identity altogether, but in seeing it for what it is: a structure I have lived inside, not the whole truth of who I am.

Once I could see that more clearly, another question began to emerge.

If identity is a structure I have lived inside, then what remains when that structure begins to loosen?

Chapter Seven

The Work of Transformation

Seeing the mechanism of the mind changed the way I understood my suffering, but it did not tell me how to live once the structure of my identity began to give way.

After my injury, even familiar social spaces began to feel different. Conversations that once would have been easy now carried a strange tension. My life's work had been interrupted. The shape my days had held for years was gone, and nothing clear had yet taken its place. People still met me through the outline of the person they had known, but inwardly that outline was already dissolving.

I smiled. I answered lightly. I tried to seem steady. But the effort was exhausting. Without the work that had once organized my life, I no longer knew what I had to offer. Beneath the surface was a quieter fear that I had lost not only direction, but value. I could feel myself trying to appear intact while something in me was still falling away.

I needed space from all of that. Not because I wanted to disappear from people entirely, but because I could feel how much energy it took to keep appearing as someone I no longer fully recognized. I needed time away from the questions, the expectations, and the subtle pressure to have some coherent account of who I was now.

When I finally had that space, something in me began to change. Alone, the pressure to be someone started to ease. It felt as though I had stepped offstage and the performance could finally end. Without anyone to answer to or perform for, the mind grew quieter and the old roles began to loosen.

So, during the months that followed, I began retreating into nature.

There were days when I paddled for hours without seeing another person. Just the quiet rhythm of the paddle entering the water, the soft wake trailing behind the boat, and the slow unfolding of the landscape around me. In that solitude, something inside me began to loosen. Without an audience, without expectations, the pressure to be someone slowly began to fall away.

I was no longer the teacher.
No longer the musician.
No longer the person people expected me to be.

Out there I was simply a body moving across water, breathing in the open air, watching the world unfold around me. I was finally looking outside of myself. Learning from nature itself.

On one particular outing, I headed out to a very remote reservoir in the middle of the Vermont woods. The water was flat and quiet when I launched the kayak, the kind of stillness that makes the surface of the lake look almost like glass. I remember the giant breath I took after I climbed into my boat and pushed off from the shore. I settled into the steady rhythm of paddling.

On the water, surrounded by stillness, I was beginning to experience a different kind of pause, a little more space between what I felt and what my mind rushed to make of it. The familiar silence settled around me and I was at peace. I was gliding across the water with every stroke, miles now from where I started, without a human in sight. I was completely alone, but so connected to everything around me.

A light breeze started to create a ripple across the surface of the lake, and the air seemed to be cooling against my skin. I looked toward the mountains and saw a dark band of clouds beginning to gather across the horizon. The change was happening quickly and within minutes a storm arrived.

Rain struck the lake so hard it looked as if the surface had begun to boil. Thousands of drops hammered the water, bouncing upward in tiny explosions. The calm surface I had been gliding across only moments earlier had transformed into something restless and alive. It almost appeared as if the rain were rising from the lake rather than falling from the sky.

The temperature continued to drop sharply. Wind pushed scattered waves across the reservoir, and the distant shoreline began to disappear behind the curtain of rain. I was sitting in the middle of open water, the wrong place to be in a storm.

I turned the kayak toward the nearest stretch of shoreline and began paddling hard. Through the white noise of the rain, I could hear a distant echo of thunder reverberating off the mountains and through the valley. Each stroke drove the paddle deeper into the water while the storm intensified around me.

Eventually I reached a narrow section of shoreline and pulled the kayak onto the rocks beneath a stand of thick trees. For a moment I hoped the branches above might offer some shelter, but the rain had already soaked me through, and nothing gave me shelter. My thin raincoat clung to my body and the cold settled in quickly. Within minutes I was shivering hard enough that I knew I was in danger of getting hypothermia. Standing still under the trees was not an option. If I didn't start moving again, the cold was going to take hold.

So, I climbed back into the kayak and pushed off once more, this time hugging the shoreline as closely as I could while rain continued to fall with almost unbelievable force. It felt like buckets of water were being dumped over my head. My breath grew heavy and each stroke began to burn in my arms and shoulders. Somewhere in the back of my mind I knew I had placed myself in a very dangerous situation.

The only thing left to do—remember to buy a better raincoat and keep paddling.

One stroke followed the next as rain hammered the lake around me. I closed my eyes and focused on each pull through the water, opening them only occasionally to make sure I wasn't drifting too far off course. Still, my mind began to spin. It first moved backward, beating me up for not checking the weather, replaying the mistake that had put me there. Then, almost instantly, it pitched forward into imagined consequence.

Was this how my story might end?
Would someone eventually find the kayak drifting out there weeks later?
Had my life already reached its final chapter?

When my hearing was injured, I thought I knew fear. But this was different. This was immediate and life-threatening.

The rhythm of my paddle began to falter. My shoulders were burning and my breath was coming in short bursts. For a moment I stopped paddling altogether and let the kayak drift beneath the weight of the rain. The storm roared around me and the lake began to heave beneath the hull.

I closed my eyes again for a moment as I was catching my breath. I listened to the rain hit the water so hard that the sound masked my tinnitus. As I lifted my head and began to paddle once more, I could see the gray ceiling of clouds churning above me. In an instant, a narrow beam of sunlight broke through and struck the water right in front of me. For a moment the storm and the sun occupied the same space. Through the column of light, the rain began to shimmer with a brilliance I had never experienced.

Raindrops struck the water and bounced upward in tiny flashes. Each one caught the sunlight for a split second before disappearing again. It looked as though the lake itself had come alive, scattering light in every direction.

I stopped paddling and just watched in awe.

A smile came across my face. I leaned back in the kayak and began laughing out loud. There I was, soaked and exhausted, sitting in the middle of a storm, yet suddenly overwhelmed by the beauty unfolding in front of me. A wave of gratitude moved through my body so strongly that for a moment it pushed every darkness aside.

I chose to take a moment and breathe. A sacred pause in the middle of the storm. I was present, probably more present than I had ever been in my life. Seeing the power of nature humbled me to my core. I floated in a strange stillness.

I thought I could see the launch site in the distance and began paddling again as I contemplated being alive, able to witness this beautiful moment. I came around a peninsula thinking I was entering the last bay where the launch was located, only to see that I wasn't even close. I had another mile to go.

The rain started getting stronger again. Then in an instant, crack! A thunderclap boomed, breaking the peace once again. The storm was not finished, and it was close.

Damn! This is my life, I thought. I had to laugh. You think the storm is done, but the lessons keep coming.

I kept paddling.

Fear had returned, but this time I met it with a smile on my face. I appreciated what the moment was teaching me. I had one job to do; just paddle and enjoy the ride. Each stroke continued to burn in my arms, but I was loving every second of it.

Gradually the storm began to move on. The rain softened, and the thunder rolled farther into the distance. Within minutes the lake had begun to calm on its own, and my kayak was once again gliding smoothly across the surface of the water.

I was cold, deeply cold, and soaked through, but the beauty of what was happening around me held my full attention. Then nature offered one more gift in the wake of the storm. A thin mist began to hover just above the surface of the lake. Thermal warmth rose into the cool air in a soft fog. It was haunting and beautiful. As it gathered around me, that warmth seemed to work its way into my bones. Nature's blanket.

My eyes were wide open. My senses were alive. My heart was still pounding from the desperate push toward shore. I had never felt so awake, so present. As the storm drifted toward the mountains, something inside me began to loosen as well. The trance of grief that had held me for so long relaxed its grip, and the simple fact of being alive came back into view.

What was in front of me did not need to mean anything more than what it was. The mist. The cold air. The stillness returning to the lake. It had all been there, waiting for me beyond the noise of my own mind.

Out there, far from the expectations of other people, I no longer had to perform the person I had been. For the first time in a long while, I was no longer absorbed in my thoughts about life.

It was enough just to be there. I was inside life again.

Chapter Eight

Non-Judgment

Not long after the storm on the lake, I found myself returning to it in my mind more than I expected. At first I assumed I was simply replaying an intense experience, but what stayed with me was not the fear. It was the strange fact that the meaning of the day had changed.

Out on the water, the storm had been dangerous. My body had every reason to react. The fear was real. The urgency was real. But when I remembered it later, what remained most vividly was not panic. It was beauty. Gratitude. Awe. The same event that could have become a story of threat had, somehow, become something else.

That unsettled me in the best way.

It made me wonder how quickly I rush to decide what everything means. Good. Bad. Fair. Unfair. Ruin. Gift. I began to see that the mind does not simply react to experience. It judges it almost immediately, then treats that judgment as though it were built into the event itself.

Around that time, I found myself returning to the old farmer story that had disturbed me so much at the beginning of my reckoning. I did not need to hear the whole parable again. What stayed with me was the question it had planted and the way it kept interrupting my certainty.

What if I do not yet know what this means?

That question had irritated me when I first encountered it. Back then I wanted clarity. I wanted my loss to mean something definite. I wanted to know whether what was happening to me was purely tragic or somehow redeemable. The story denied me that clean conclusion. Now, after months of watching the mind form stories, gather evidence, and turn pain into identity, that same question began softening something in me.

I had already learned how to pause. I could sometimes interrupt the reflex long enough to notice what was happening in me. But pausing was not the same as loosening the verdict that usually followed. I could stop the momentum for a breath and still remain trapped inside a strong conclusion about what the moment meant. Something else had to soften too.

Once I could pause inside experience, the next task was learning not to grade every moment so quickly as good or bad. I was beginning to see how quickly the mind becomes a judge. The moment something hurts, it declares it wrong. The moment something pleases me, it becomes good. If something threatens my plans, my identity, or my sense of control, the mind does not simply notice the discomfort. It hands down a sentence.

The judge in my mind was not malicious. It was trying to protect me. It wanted the world sorted quickly so I could move toward safety and away from pain. In that sense, judgment was not the enemy. It was a primitive form of care, but it moved too quickly. It escalated too fast. It mistook its first reading of the moment for the truth of the moment.

That was what I had started feeling in myself after the storm. The pause could keep me from disappearing completely into the reflex, but non-judgment was something different. It was the refusal to let the first interpretation become the final word.

This is why I have come to think of equanimity not as detachment, but as non-escalation.

It does not mean the feeling is not real. It does not mean I stop caring. It means I do not have to add a sentence to the feeling so quickly. I do not have to turn pain into prophecy. I do not have to turn discomfort into identity. I do not have to decide, in the first surge of experience, what the event means for the rest of my life.

That distinction changed everything.

The loss of my hearing was painful enough. But once the mind declared it ruin, once it treated the event as proof that life had collapsed beyond repair, the pain deepened into something much harder to carry. The suffering was no longer only in what had happened. It was in the speed with which I judged what had happened and the certainty with which I believed my own verdict.

Equanimity opened a different possibility. Not that the loss was good. Not that it was secretly a blessing. But that I did not yet know everything it would become. That I could meet it without turning it immediately into final meaning.

That softening changed the inner atmosphere.

The body did not have to brace as hard, because the mind was no longer shouting an emergency into the nervous system. The feeling could still be intense, but it moved through more cleanly when judgment did not keep grabbing it and turning it into a case. The event remained real. The charge remained real. What changed was the extra layer of escalation.

For most of my life, my reflex had been to fix, interpret, and name. If something hurt, I wanted to know what was wrong and what needed to change. If something felt good, I wanted to preserve it. Equanimity did not erase that habit overnight, but it gave me another way of meeting what was happening.

Instead of asking how do I get rid of this? I could ask what happens if I let this be here for one breath before I decide what it means?

That was a different kind of strength.

Thich Nhat Hanh writes about equanimity as freedom from grasping and pushing away. That language helped me, but only after I had already begun feeling the truth of it in my own body. The system wants to cling to what feels pleasant and recoil from what feels painful. The mind joins in by turning those movements into narrative. Equanimity interrupts that process just enough for a different relationship to emerge.

Not the absence of feeling.
Not the end of preference.
Just less compulsion.

That was the key. Equanimity did not make me passive. It made me less immediately reactive. It let me stay with the moment long enough for a little more honesty to enter.

And that honesty led me back into language.

I continued journaling, but the writing was changing. The page was no longer only a place to document suffering. It was becoming a place to test perception itself. I started playing with words the way I once played with sound, listening for what happened when I shifted the angle of a phrase. I was still grieving, still disoriented, still carrying the injury every day. But something creative began moving again inside the very terrain I had once assumed was only ruin.

That is when I found the word **Upekkhā**.

It came out of Buddhist teachings on equanimity, and the word itself landed in me like a tone I had been waiting to hear. It did not solve anything. It did not erase the pain. But it gave the shift a sound, a shape, a center of gravity. I began writing lyrics, not because I had transcended the suffering, but because I was beginning to witness it differently.

At first I was still writing from inside the fracture:

> **[Verse 1]**
> It started with a sound that didn't feel right,
> just hung in the air, like a beam of light
> It fills my mind with a shimmer so bright
> Hiding the music that has brought delight
> I tried to explain it, tame it, contain it.
> Told myself it would fade, but it chose to stay
> Silence I lost, with my story in tow.
> Once that cracked, all the questions took hold.

That verse still carried the old reflex. The need to explain. The urge to contain. The instinct to decide too quickly what had happened and what it meant. But as the writing continued, the center of gravity began shifting. The song started teaching me what experience itself was trying to teach me.

Not good.
Not bad.
Just real.

That phrase did not come from detachment. It came from contact. It came from letting the experience be present before grading it. The more I lived with that orientation, the more I could feel the difference between suppressing emotion and allowing emotion to move without turning it into identity.

That is why the next turn in the song mattered so much to me.

> **[Verse 2]**
> How do I fix this? When will it stop?
> A part of me broke, how do I get it back?
> It is here to stay, and the change has begun.
> To meet it the same means the work is never done.
> What if it's not broken? What if I just bend?
> What if the story I've been telling has come to an end?
> I thought I was the sound, the tone, the role.
> But maybe I'm something deeper,
> the pulse of a soul.

What moved me in those lines was not the suggestion that the loss was secretly good. It was the possibility that I had been too quick to call it final in the way I first did. Equanimity was not replacing grief with positivity. It was replacing judgment with a wider field of view.

Pema Chödrön writes often about this kind of staying, the willingness to remain present with what hurts without immediately fleeing, numbing, or turning away. That felt true to me. Allowing is not collapse. It is contact. It is staying close enough to experience that it can reveal more of itself before the mind seals it shut with verdict.

> **[Pre-Chorus]**
> When the noise fills my head,
> And I can't find the ground,
> I don't push it away,
> I don't run from the sound...

Those lines mattered to me because they named the shift more simply than I could explain it. I was no longer trying to overpower the experience or outrun it. I was learning to remain with it long enough for the judgment around it to soften.

The pause helped me see that I was reacting.
Non-judgment helped me stop turning the reaction into a conclusion.

The pause interrupted the momentum of the reaction. Equanimity kept me from turning that reaction into certainty.

Up to this point, I had been learning how the reflex works, how the body tightens, how story forms, how evidence reinforces perception, how identity wraps itself around interpretation, and how practice begins through return. What was changing now was subtler. The lens itself was beginning to soften.

Once the lens softened, experience changed.

Not because life suddenly became gentle.
Because I stopped meeting everything with a verdict.

That shift did not make me wise overnight. I still judged. I still reacted. I still wanted clarity more quickly than life could offer it. But the judge had been exposed. I could feel when it entered the room. I could sense how it tried to help by deciding too fast. And because I could sense it, I did not have to obey it every time.

It showed up in the smallest moments. A wave of sadness. A difficult conversation. A memory that reopened pain. A surge of shame. Instead of instantly sorting the feeling into right or wrong, progress or failure, healing or collapse, I could sometimes just notice it.

Here is grief.
Here is fear.
Here is disappointment.
Here is relief.

Not a verdict.
A visitation.

That simple shift changed my relationship to inner life. Emotion stopped being an enemy and became information. The judge stopped being a villain and became something I could understand: a protector trying to restore order too quickly. Once I saw that, I could meet even judgment itself with a little more patience.

We are not only learning to see without judgment.
We are learning to see even our judgment without judgment.

That was a subtle but important turn. If I judged my judging, the loop simply changed costumes. But if I could notice the judge arising as part of the human machinery of protection, something softened. The system no longer had to defend itself quite so hard.

By the time I reached the final verse of the song, this was the movement I could hear in it.

> **[Verse 3]**
> The sound's still here, like breath, like time.
> I stopped asking why, and started making it mine.
> Not good, not bad, just real, just now.
> No need to fix it. Just learn how.
> My old story is done. I laid it down.
> And in its place, I found Upekkhā's crown.
> I'm not chasing quiet. I'm not holding back.
> I'm walking forward on a brand-new track.
> Not good. Not bad.
> Just present in awe.
> That's how I found,
> U-pek-khā

The song did not resolve my life. But it showed me that awareness could hold pain without immediately turning it into a prison. It showed me that judgment was not the only possible response to experience. It showed me that the mind could loosen its grip without losing contact with what was real. That, to me, is the beginning of equanimity.

Not a lofty spiritual state.
Not emotional flatness.
Not distance from life.

A steadier way of being touched by life without being carried off by the first verdict that rises in the mind.

From there, something else began to change too. Once experience no longer had to be sorted so quickly into good and bad, the whole field of perception began opening. I could start noticing not only what I felt, but how I was seeing.

That change in seeing began reshaping everything.

Chapter Nine

Training the Interpretive Lens

Non-judgment opened the door, but it did not immediately free me from the habits of perception I had spent years rehearsing. I still had to see how repetition had trained the lens through which I met the world. By the time I left teaching, I was no longer meeting each day with fresh eyes.

I did not understand that at first. I thought I was simply tired, frustrated, burned out by the ordinary pressures of work. A difficult meeting here. A strained interaction there. A policy that felt disconnected from the reality of the classroom. A conversation that left a residue behind. Each moment seemed manageable on its own, but the nervous system keeps records even when the mind insists everything is fine. What I did not see at the time was how much I was carrying forward from one day into the next.

Anyone who has taken a long summer drive knows what eventually happens to the windshield. Bugs strike the glass at highway speed. Some leave a faint mark. Others explode into thick splatters that bake in the sun. The wipers drag across them, trying to clear the view, but often all they do is smear the impact into stubborn streaks. At first you barely notice. Then, mile after mile, the residue accumulates, and before long the road ahead is still there, but you are no longer seeing it cleanly.

That was what my teaching life had become.

Each difficult meeting was another splatter. Each crossed boundary another smear. Each disappointment another layer of residue on the glass. Most of the time I simply kept driving. I moved from one problem to the next, trying to keep going, assuming the view was still clear enough. But the residue never really disappeared. It stayed there quietly, shaping how the next moment would be seen.

Over time I stopped seeing the full landscape of my work. I no longer noticed the many moments of humor, beauty, and connection that had once made teaching feel alive. They were still there, but my attention had been captured by what had accumulated on the glass. The lens had been trained. The mind had learned where to look.

That is the danger of a trained lens. It does not simply distort what you see. It begins deciding what stands out. And once that happens, the world starts confirming the way you have already been prepared to see it.

By the final stretch of my teaching career, I was no longer responding to each day as a new day. I was looking through the residue of old conflict, fatigue, and disappointment. The more often certain experiences landed with charge, the more easily the next moment was interpreted through the same imprint. That is how perception gets conditioned. A reaction that once belonged to one moment begins shaping the meaning of the next.

Eventually the strain reached a point where the pattern became impossible to ignore. One particular day at school unfolded as a string of conflicts from the moment I arrived until the moment I left. What struck me most was not only the tension itself, but the absence of empathy surrounding it. Conversations felt defensive on every side. Everyone seemed to be protecting their own ground, and accountability dissolved into noise.

By the end of that day, I got into my car and decided I was done.

At the time, it felt like I was taking control, using what little agency I had left. But the truth was simpler and harder. My system had reached capacity. What I had been calling resilience had slowly become exhaustion. Leaving was not a carefully reasoned decision. It was the response of a nervous system that had run out of room.

Months later, my hearing injury arrived and completed the collapse. It was the final rupture, the closing act of a life I could no longer sustain. When that happened, everything went quiet. There was nothing left to fix. No institution to manage. No role to perform. No next meeting waiting to be survived.

For the first time in years, I just listened. To the ringing. To the ache of everything that had been lost. To what remained when the machinery finally stopped.

In that stillness, I began sensing something unfamiliar. It was not comfort, not yet, but it was not despair either. It was a steadier presence beneath the panic of my thoughts. A way of seeing that was not so entangled with the story I had been telling.

At first it felt like surrender. Later I would understand it differently. It felt like a return to what was actually here.

Five simple words began circling in my mind.

It is what it is.

I used to hear that phrase as resignation, as if it meant giving up or no longer caring. But in that moment it began to mean something else. It was not a shrug. It was a release from arguing with what had already happened. Not what I wanted. Not what I feared. Just what was.

That was my first real taste of radical acceptance.

Radical acceptance is not approval. It does not mean I like what happened or stop grieving it. It means I stop fighting reality as though my refusal will somehow undo it. It means grief is allowed to be grief without immediately becoming a prophecy about the future. It means pain can stay pain without being forced into a larger verdict about the whole of life.

Once I began to understand this, the windshield image shifted in my mind.

For years I had been trapped behind the glass, squinting through old residue and mistaking the distortion for reality itself. Then the image changed. I rolled down the window and stuck my head out.

The bugs were still there. The windshield was still marked. The past had not vanished. But the angle changed. For a moment, I was no longer mistaking the residue for the road itself. I could see the marks as marks, the evidence of where I had been, not a prophecy about where I was going.

That mattered.

I cannot erase my past in a single breath. I cannot unlive my conditioning. But I can sometimes choose where to place my attention. I can notice when old residue is shaping the moment. I can remember that not everything appearing in front of me belongs entirely to what is in front of me. Sometimes the shift is as simple as rolling down the window and sticking my head out long enough to get a different view.

Around that time, a friend texted me a single word she had been using as a kind of inner orientation.

Sweetness.

At first it struck me as strange. Was she talking about kindness? Gentleness? Compassion? I was not sure. But the more I sat with it, the more it opened something in me. I became curious whether I could meet experience through a different tone altogether. Not denial. Not forced positivity. Just a different posture. I was not trying to replace one thought with another. I was trying to alter the tone with which I met the experience itself.

Could I meet the moment with sweetness?

My years as a conductor had taught me something I only later recognized as useful outside music. A gesture does not read as authentic unless it emerges from the body first. You cannot ask an ensemble for warmth, urgency, or tenderness through choreography alone. The signal has to be felt before it can be expressed. If I wanted the sound to open, something in me had to open first. If I wanted gentleness, my body had to know gentleness. Otherwise, the gesture was accurate but hollow.

So, I approached sweetness that way. Not as an idea to admire, but as a filter to inhabit.

I softened my face. Slowed my pace. Relaxed my jaw. Let my gaze become a little gentler. I let myself imagine, just for a moment, what sweetness might feel like in the body before I asked it to shape the mind. I was not pretending life was sweet. I was altering the filter through which I was meeting it.

Something subtle happened. My chest softened. My attention widened. My tone changed. I began listening more deeply. A small conflict later that day gave me a chance to test it. Instead of sharpening immediately, I slowed down. Instead of bracing, I stayed present. Compassion entered the room more easily. The situation itself did not disappear, but the way I met it changed the whole field around it.

That was important for me to learn. Retraining perception did not begin as a grand idea. It began as a change in posture, breath, expression, and tone. The lens could be re-aimed.

That was when "begin again" took on a more practical meaning for me. It stopped sounding inspirational and started becoming perceptual. To begin again was not to forget the past. It was to stop letting the past do all the seeing.

There is a Zen phrase for this, beginner's mind. Not innocence. Not naivete. A willingness to meet the moment without handing the whole interpretation over to old certainty. A willingness to admit that this moment may not be identical to the last one, even if it resembles it. Beginning again, in that sense, was not a performance of optimism. It was a way of meeting the moment with fresh eyes.

That kind of vision is not automatic. It has to be practiced.

Around this same time, my daughter and I were both carrying a great deal of grief. We began noticing something about it together. Grief did not stay still. It moved in waves. It gathered, lifted, broke, and returned. Some days it was barely noticeable. Other days it came crashing back with force.

In jest, we gave it a name.

Lolita.

Naming it did not solve anything, but it changed our relationship to it. It turned the feeling into weather rather than identity. When one of us said, "Lolita's back," what we really meant was that the wave was here again. Not forever. Not as a final truth. Just here, moving through.

That was one of the clearest ways impermanence began teaching me from the inside.

Pain does not last in the way the mind first claims it will. It ebbs. It swells. It returns. It changes shape. Even grief, which can feel so absolute when it arrives, does not hold a single form. It moves through seasons, through bodies, through memory, through time. That did not make it less real. It made it less final.

That mattered, because once I could feel grief as movement rather than identity, something larger came into view. Life is full of endings, but endings are never the whole story. They create openings too. They clear space. They alter the landscape. They ask for a new way of seeing. What the mind first calls loss may also be the beginning of something it cannot yet recognize.

That changed the atmosphere around suffering.

Instead of saying, *This is me now*, I could sometimes say, *This is here now.* That small difference gave me room to breathe. Thoughts formed. Emotion swelled. A wave broke. Something quieter returned. Some waves were heavy. Some gentle. Some frightening. Some strangely beautiful. But none of them were permanent. None of them had to define me.

The lens of equanimity is not about stopping the storm. It is about learning to stand there steadily enough to watch the storm move through without becoming the storm itself.

Once I could feel this in my own experience, I began responding differently.

Earlier in my reckoning, every ending had folded into the same narrative of decline. My career, my hearing, my sense of self, all of it seemed to point toward diminishment. Later, once the lens softened, something quieter became visible. These were not only losses. They were transitions. Movements in a larger cycle I had not known how to recognize while I was still fighting them.

Impermanence was not punishing me.

It was reshaping me.

That realization did not erase the grief. It did not make change easy. But it changed the stance from which I met change. I no longer had to force every experience into proof that life was getting smaller. Sometimes what felt like ending was also clearing. Sometimes what disappeared left room for something I could not yet imagine.

This is where effort itself had to change. For most of my life, effort meant pushing harder, tightening, insisting, trying to force the result I wanted. But there is another kind of effort, one that does not bully the moment into submission. In Buddhist language, this is closer to Right Effort, not strain, but the right kind of energy applied in the right place. Not more force. Better alignment.

Each time I noticed the residue, softened instead of braced, re-aimed instead of reacted, and began again, the system was being retrained.

What I began to notice was subtle but unmistakable. The more I loosened the grip of the judge in my mind, the more the next moment was met with balance. Conflict still appeared. Difficulty still arrived. But it no longer landed in exactly the same way. Something in me had stopped rushing so quickly to verdict, and because of that, the lens itself began to clear.

That is how new conditioning begins.

The old pattern had been built through repetition, through moments of charge being met with the same reflex over and over again. But the opposite is also true. When a new conflict appears and I can feel it, see it, take a breath, and stay with it long enough to let it reveal itself, the old machine does not fire in the same way. The buttons are still there, but they no longer get pressed so easily, because something in me has been unplugged from the system that used to react automatically.

The conflict is still real. The sensation is still real. But now there is more room around it. More balance. More honesty. I am no longer meeting the moment only through the residue of the past. I am meeting it with a lens that is slowly being cleared by practice.

That is what retraining started to mean for me. Not becoming invulnerable. Not never reacting again. But meeting the next moment in a way that does not automatically strengthen the old groove.

Chapter Ten

Begin Again

As the lens softened, the question changed from how to escape life to how to re-enter it differently. In the months after my reckoning, returning to ordinary life felt unfamiliar in a way I had not expected.

From the outside, nothing had changed. People still moved through their days with the same routines. Conversations followed familiar patterns. Interactions opened and closed with the same polite rhythm they always had. The world continued forward as though nothing unusual had happened.

Yet something in the way I was seeing it had shifted.

Once my perceptions began to soften, certain patterns became difficult to ignore. Reactions that once seemed invisible began to stand out in quiet ways. A defensive tone could enter a conversation before anyone named it. Someone could offer an opinion with complete certainty even though the answer was not clear. A room could slowly fill with tension simply because one person's frustration had drifted across the group and everyone else had begun adjusting around it.

At first I found myself watching these moments almost the way you watch a scene unfold on a stage. The choreography was familiar, but I had never seen it quite so plainly. People stepped into roles without realizing they were doing it. One person became the expert. Another became the fixer. Someone else assumed the quiet responsibility of smoothing the interaction so everything could continue without disruption.

For a brief time, it even felt as though awareness had placed me slightly outside the system, as though I were observing something I was no longer a part of.

But that impression did not last long.

The same reflexes were still alive in me. I could feel the urge to defend a position the moment my ideas were questioned. I could feel the subtle pull toward approval when a conversation drifted toward judgment. I noticed how quickly my mind began forming responses before the other person had finished speaking. Seeing the pattern in others simply made it harder to ignore it in myself.

That mattered, because I did not want awareness to become another disguise for separation. I did not want to become the person standing outside the room, silently diagnosing everyone else while pretending I had somehow moved beyond the same machinery. That would have been just another identity, another story the mind could use to protect itself.

What I was learning was not how to rise above ordinary life.

I was learning how to enter it differently.

That difference was subtle, but decisive. In the past, so much of social life had been organized around performance. Trying to seem competent. Trying to be liked. Trying to say the right thing, land in the right place, hold my shape inside the expectations of the room. Even when I thought I was being sincere, some part of me was often still arranging itself to fit the role I believed the moment required.

After the reckoning, that old performance began to feel much harder to sustain. At first this was disorienting. I no longer wanted to explain myself all the time, but I also did not know what it meant to simply be with people without quietly managing how I was being perceived. I had spent so long trying to become someone in the eyes of others that I had not fully learned how to participate without using every interaction to confirm or defend a self.

That, I think, is one of the deeper tasks of beginning again.

Not disappearing from life.
Not becoming detached from people.
Not floating above the room in private enlightenment.

Participating without performance.

It is one thing to speak of participating without performance. It is another to recognize what the people closest to you have to live with while you are learning how. Transformation may be inward, but it is rarely private. The need for solitude, the shedding of identity, the hours I spent writing or disappearing into nature were not happening in isolation. My family was living inside the weather of my reckoning with me.

I was fortunate. The people closest to me seemed to know, almost instinctively, how to give me space without withdrawing their love. My wife, in particular, remained steady while I was anything but. She gave me room to unravel, to question, to go quiet, and to return in my own time. As old roles fell away, I became self-absorbed in ways I could sometimes see but not always interrupt. I had less certainty, less steadiness, less of the familiar self I had once brought into the room. There were stretches when all I seemed to carry was grief, reflection, and the need to be alone. Still, they all remained. They adjusted. They carried responsibilities I could no longer hold. They kept meeting me as I was, even when who I was had become unclear.

That changed the way I saw them. As the pressure to rebuild myself began to ease, so did the pressure I had unconsciously placed on others. I was no longer holding the people I loved against the expectations of the life that had collapsed. I was beginning to see them more as they were. Not for what they could fix, confirm, or protect in me, but for the steadiness of their presence, the grace of their patience, and the quiet generosity of those who made room for me to become unfamiliar and did not turn away. Gratitude grew there. So did humility. By the time I began learning how to participate without performance, I had already been given my first lesson in it at home.

For me, this began in very small ways. I noticed the urge to impress and did not immediately obey it. I noticed the impulse to smooth over discomfort too quickly and let the silence breathe for another moment. I noticed the reflex to make a clever point, to prove I understood something, to subtly establish myself in the room, and instead I tried simply listening.

Listening without preparing. Listening without immediately translating everything into what it meant about me. Listening without using the other person's words as raw material for my next reply.

This turned out to be much harder than it sounds. It also turned out to be one of the most practical forms of awareness I had encountered.

There is a particular relief that comes when you no longer need every interaction to stabilize identity. A conversation can remain a conversation. A disagreement can remain a disagreement. A moment of awkwardness does not have to become a referendum on who you are. When that pressure eases, something else becomes possible. Curiosity returns. Humor returns. Even tenderness returns, because the self is no longer taking up the entire field.

This did not mean I stopped caring what people thought. It did not mean old sensitivities vanished. It meant they no longer carried quite the same authority. I could feel the reflex begin and sometimes, not always, remain in the room without letting it run the whole exchange.

Again and again, I found myself returning to the same quiet instruction.

Begin again.

The phrase had first come to me through meditation, but by then I could feel how much larger it was. It was not just something to do with closed eyes and a cushion. It belonged in kitchens, meetings, car rides, phone calls, ordinary conversations, tense pauses, passing irritations, and small moments of contact with other human beings.

Whenever the mind drifted into defense, performance, resentment, or self-consciousness, the invitation was the same. Notice what has happened. Take a breath. Begin again from here. What surprised me most was the gentleness embedded in the instruction. The moment awareness returned was not treated as failure. It was treated as the point of the practice.

That changed the way I related to social friction. If I got hooked by someone's tone, I did not have to turn that into proof that I was still broken or still reactive or still not far enough along. If I caught myself performing, it was not a moral failure. It was a human reflex. The work was simply to notice it and return.

That return began teaching me something I could never have learned through analysis alone. The nervous system does not change because you shame it into submission. It changes through repeated contact with a new experience. Each time a charged moment arrived, and I met it with a little more space, a little less defense, a little less performance, something in me learned that the old response was no longer the only response available. This is where humility became essential.

There is no chapter of growth after which one becomes permanently free from awkwardness, self-protection, or emotional weather. I still get pulled. I still misread people. I still hear criticism where there may only be difference. I still notice old desires to be admired, understood, agreed with, or reassured. The difference is not that those reflexes are gone. The difference is that they no longer mean the same thing.

They do not automatically mean I am lost.
They do not automatically mean I have failed.
They do not automatically mean I need to rebuild the old machinery.

Sometimes they mean only that I am a human being in contact with other human beings, carrying a nervous system with a history. That recognition softened me. It also made other people easier to meet.

Once I stopped needing to stand apart from them, I could feel more clearly that what I was witnessing in others was not so different from what I had witnessed in myself. The certainty. The self-protection. The quick defenses. The need to be right. The need to be seen in a certain light. Underneath all of it was vulnerability. Underneath much of that vulnerability was fear. And underneath much of that fear was the same thing I knew intimately in myself: the strain of trying to remain intact inside a world that keeps changing.

That realization did not make me passive. It made me less eager to escalate.

Compassion, I found, is not a performance of niceness. It is the natural result of seeing more accurately. Once I could feel how much effort goes into defending a self, both in myself and in others, I no longer wanted every difficult moment to end in victory. Sometimes what mattered more was remaining human inside it. That changed how I understood participation.

I used to think participation meant contributing, proving, leading, helping, producing something useful, or at least holding my place convincingly enough that I would not disappear. Now I think participation is something simpler and harder. It is staying in relationship with what is here without turning away and without turning the whole moment into a stage for self-construction.

To participate is to let life touch you and still remain present.

A conversation with someone you love.
A disagreement that does not need to become war.
A chore done without resentment.
A silence that does not need immediate filling.
A morning cup of coffee held with full attention.
An apology made without collapse.
A room entered without needing to manage every impression.
A shared laugh that is not doing any work except being real.

These moments do not look dramatic. They rarely announce themselves as transformation. But this, more and more, is where beginning again has come to live for me. Not in grand reinvention. In ordinary contact. In the decision to return to the moment as it is, and to meet the people in it without asking them to stabilize my identity.

This is what it means, for me, to re-enter life with a changed lens.

Not as someone who has figured it all out.
Not as someone who has transcended the old reflexes.
Not as someone standing above the ordinary world.

As someone willing to be in it.
To notice.
To soften.
To participate.
To begin again in the middle of real human contact.

And perhaps that is where the path becomes most honest. Not when awareness takes us away from life, but when it returns us to life with less armor, less performance, and a little more room to be here together.

Chapter Eleven

Staying in Tune

Re-entry was not a final breakthrough. It became a daily practice of drift, return, and retraining. At some point along the path of trying to understand the mind, a quieter realization begins to settle in.

Seeing the mechanism of our reactions can feel liberating at first. What once seemed mysterious starts to become visible. Sensation arises. The mind interprets. The body reacts. Before long, an entire emotional reality can form around a story written in a fraction of a second. What once felt like truth begins to reveal itself as process.

That matters. To see the reflex is no small thing. For many of us, it is the first real interruption of a life lived on autopilot. But seeing the pattern is not the same as being free of it. Awareness gave me a foothold, but it did not automatically teach me how to live. I could name what was happening and still be carried by it. I could understand the loop and still find myself inside it on an ordinary Tuesday afternoon, irritated by something small, defending a position that did not need defending, or drifting so far into thought that the moment itself had gone missing.

Why?

Because conditioning runs deeper than insight alone.

The nervous system was shaped for survival, not reflection. Long before the modern world appeared, the human organism learned to move quickly toward what felt rewarding and away from what felt threatening. Attraction and aversion became the basic grammar of our reactions. That reflex helped us survive.

But that ancient wiring now operates inside a culture that magnifies it constantly. If something feels dull, uncertain, uncomfortable, or unresolved, an easier distraction is always close at hand. Another source of relief is always available. Another hit of certainty, validation, entertainment, or control can usually be found in seconds.

Over time, this shapes more than habit. It shapes our posture toward life itself.

We begin to consume experience the way we consume everything else. We skim. We sort. We sample. We ask whether a moment is pleasing, useful, validating, or easy to digest. We want payoff. We want relief. We want certainty. We want the emotional equivalent of fast delivery.

The reflexive mind becomes a consumer of life.

I think that is part of why real change is so difficult. It is not only that the reflex is fast. It is that we have been trained to live inside its logic. We have become accustomed to meeting experience by judging it immediately. If something feels unresolved, we assume it is a problem. If it feels painful, we assume it should be removed. If it does not reward us quickly, we struggle to stay in contact with it at all.

Yet almost everything of value in a human life asks something very different of us. Trust deepens slowly. Understanding matures slowly. Love steadies slowly. Healing takes hold slowly. None of these can be consumed on demand. They emerge through a process that asks for patience, repetition, revision, and the willingness to remain in relationship with what is unfinished.

That is why creative practice matters so much. Not because it makes us artistic, but because it forms us over time.

Anyone who has spent serious time with an instrument eventually discovers that growth does not come from demanding immediate reward. Practice is often repetitive, awkward, and strangely unglamorous. Progress is slow. Mistakes are constant. The gap between what we want to do and what we can actually do can feel enormous. It is easy to become frustrated, easy to judge ourselves, easy to want some proof that all this effort is leading somewhere.

But something changes if we stay with it.

We stop asking every moment to justify itself. We begin listening more closely. The hand learns through repetition. The ear grows more sensitive. Timing settles. The body begins to trust the process. What once felt like failure becomes part of formation.

Music taught me this long before I had language for it. A wrong note is not the end of the piece. A missed entrance is not proof that I should quit. It is feedback. Information. A chance to listen, adjust, and return. The practice is not to avoid every wobble. The practice is to keep coming back to the deeper tone beneath the wobble.

Living well has started to feel like that.

Not the elimination of tension, but the willingness to listen closely enough to sense when something is off and to adjust without violence. When I am out of alignment with myself, with another person, or with the moment I am in, life develops that same inner wobble. Dissonance appears, and with it the old reflex to tighten, defend, or force. But when I return with patience, when I stop consuming the moment and begin working with it, something settles. The dissonance softens. The deeper tone comes through.

This is where the work becomes very ordinary.

It is one thing to speak about equanimity, awareness, or acceptance in the abstract. It is another thing entirely to practice them while unloading the dishwasher in a bad mood, while feeling misunderstood by someone you love, while sitting in traffic, while answering an email you do not want to answer, while waking with a heaviness you cannot explain.

Most of the path is lived there.

I used to imagine that growth would arrive as some cleaner, more elevated version of myself. Instead, it has shown up as smaller things. Catching the moment when my tone sharpens and softening it before it lands. Noticing the urge to withdraw and staying in the conversation a little longer. Feeling the body tighten when I want to be right, then taking a breath before I speak. Realizing halfway through a familiar mental loop that I have drifted and quietly coming back to what is actually here.

None of that looks dramatic.

That is part of its honesty.

The work continues in daily behavior. In how I speak to my wife when I am tired. In whether I rush through a conversation or actually listen. In whether I let frustration become atmosphere in a room. In whether I do the dishes with resentment or with attention. In whether I relate to the day as something to get through or something to participate in.

This is where I have had to become more humble.

There is no permanent arrival. No final state after which one becomes incapable of irritation, pettiness, self-importance, or drift. I still get hooked. I still become LIT. I still misread tone. I still feel old sensitivities rise up in me. I still reach for control when I feel uncertain. I still want reassurance faster than life can honestly give it.

The difference is not that those tendencies have vanished. The difference is that they no longer carry the same authority. They do not automatically mean I am lost, that I have failed, or that I need to rebuild the old machinery. Often they mean only that I am human, that I have a nervous system with a history, and that this moment is another chance to listen more carefully.

That is what begin again has come to mean for me now. Not an idea. Not a slogan. A way of returning when I drift.

Notice when you have drifted.
Return without punishment.
Begin again

That is the sustainable form of it.

Not because the mind stops wandering, but because the return becomes more familiar than the panic about wandering. Not because the old conditioning disappears, but because it loses some of its power when it is met repeatedly with attention rather than obedience. Each time I return with awareness instead of obedience, I am not only interrupting the old pattern. I am teaching the lens, through repetition, that another way of seeing is possible.

Over time, I began noticing that emotional drift often announced itself first not as thought, but as mood. Before I had words for what was happening, I could usually feel the change in the atmosphere within me.

Mood, I have found, is often the earliest sign that I have drifted out of relationship with the moment. Not something to judge, but something to listen to. A tightening in the chest. A brittle quality in my thoughts. A sense of speed, pressure, or rehearsed irritation. Those are usually the first signals that I have moved back under the influence of an old pattern.

If awareness is the tuner, mood is often the first sign that I have drifted out of tune.

That does not mean every bad mood is a problem to solve. It means mood can tell the truth faster than language does. It can show me that something in me has narrowed, hardened, or slipped off center. From there, the question is no longer how to get rid of it as quickly as possible, but what it would mean to come back into tune.

Sometimes the answer is a breath.
Sometimes it is silence.
Sometimes it is an apology.
Sometimes it is rest.
Sometimes it is simply not believing the first thought that arrives.

That is why the work feels less dramatic to me now than it once did. Less like spiritual breakthrough. More like maintenance of relationship.

A musician does not tune an instrument once and expect it to stay that way forever. Weather changes. Strings stretch. Rooms differ. The ear has to keep returning. Human life is not so different. Conditions shift. Stress accumulates. Old fears resurface. New demands appear. We drift. Then we listen again.

That, to me, is what staying in tune means.

Not perfection.
Not control.
Not a life without drift.

A life of listening, participation, adjustment, and return until something truer begins to ring.

When it does, something larger than the original struggle can appear. Not because the difficulty vanished, but because I came into better relationship with it. The ordinary moment stops being something to consume or endure and becomes something I can actually inhabit.

A walk.
A meal.
A hard conversation.
A silence.
A familiar chore.
A passing wave of sadness.
A moment of laughter that arrives without effort.

These are not interruptions to the path.

They are the path.

For a human life, that is enough.

Chapter Twelve

Living in the Unknown

Even after the return, life did not become clear. It became more livable without certainty.

There is often a strange emotional hangover. A dull ache that comes and goes. The world looks too quiet and too intense at the same time. For me, it felt as if my ship had been torn apart by a tsunami and I had been left floating alone in open water.

I wasn't drowning.

But nothing felt familiar.

No map.
No compass.
Just the rise and fall of the waves.

At first, that kind of openness felt deeply uncomfortable. The mind does not love a life it cannot organize. It wants a plan. It wants a role. It wants a direction it can point to and call progress. It wants to know what comes next, and it wants to know now.

When no clear answer appeared, I did what many of us do. I began searching for another plan to replace the old one. My mind scanned for a new identity, a new goal, some fresh direction that could restore the feeling of forward motion. But nothing arrived that way. The harder I searched for the next chapter of my life, the more obvious it became that the old engine had simply gone quiet.

That silence was harder to bear than I expected.

For most of my life, movement itself had been enough to create the feeling that life was progressing toward something meaningful. The next rehearsal. The next semester. The next goal. The next obligation. The future sat just ahead of me, quietly organizing everything around it.

Without those structures in place, life felt wide open.

That openness was not immediately peaceful. It was disorienting. Without a script to follow, I found myself asking a question I had never seriously considered before.

If the old story no longer determines my direction, how do I choose how to live?

The mind wanted that question answered quickly. It kept reaching for certainty the way a frightened body reaches for an exit. But over time I began to see that not every season of life is asking to be solved.

Some are asking to be grieved.
Some are asking to be lived.
Some are asking for the old form to end before the new one appears.

What made this difficult was not only uncertainty itself. It was how deeply I had been trained to treat the present moment as a steppingstone toward an imagined future. "Forward" had always felt self-evident to me, as if life were naturally carrying me toward somewhere better, and as if my task were simply to manage the movement well enough.

Standing inside the quiet that followed my reckoning, something about that began to loosen.

The future had always existed mostly in thought. It gave the present a certain shape, but it was still imagination. Life itself had only ever been happening here, in the actual moment being lived.

That did not mean planning became meaningless. Plans still matter. Goals still matter. They help us organize our energy and move toward what we care about.

What changed for me was where those plans grew from.

Instead of trying to invent a future identity and force my life toward it, I began to notice how direction often arises from the curiosity already alive in the present moment. When something genuinely captures our attention, we move toward it. We explore it. The exploration suggests the next step, and the next one after that.

Plans begin to form not as a way of forcing life into a predetermined shape, but as a way of supporting something that is already unfolding.

That changed everything.

I had spent so much of my life assuming that purpose would announce itself as certainty, as if clarity should come first and action second. What I slowly began to discover was almost the reverse. Curiosity came first. Attention came first. A small honest movement came first. The larger shape only became visible afterward.

That was a humbling realization.

It meant I did not need to solve my whole life in order to take one real step.

I only needed enough awareness to notice what felt quietly alive.

A sentence that stayed with me.
A page I wanted to write.
A conversation that opened something.
A small pleasure that felt honest.
A direction that did not feel urgent, but true.

These did not look dramatic.

They looked almost too small to trust.

But over time, I began to see that this is how a life reforms after disruption. Not through a grand declaration. Through the next honest step taken without leaving yourself behind.

That is what curiosity gave me.

Not a map.
A compass.

When the mind stopped trying to force life into the shape of a plan, a quieter form of movement began to appear. Curiosity replaced urgency. Attention replaced anticipation. The day no longer felt like a problem to solve. It became something to participate in.

That participation did not erase uncertainty. It changed my relationship to it.

The unknown no longer felt only like absence. It began to feel like openness.

Some mornings I still woke with a fog I could not explain. Not a crisis. Just a quiet unease, an echo of the older self who believed safety required certainty. When that happened, I tried not to turn the feeling into prophecy. I moved gently. I wrote. I walked. I did the dishes. I let the day begin without demanding that it explain itself.

The unease was not always a sign that something was wrong.

Sometimes it was only residue.
A nervous system remembering what it once believed.
A body asking for gentleness rather than instruction.

Each time I softened, breathed, and returned, I taught myself something new.

The unknown does not always need to be solved.

It can be felt.

That insight changed the texture of daily life. I began listening more closely. Not for a grand mission, but for alignment. Not what felt impressive. What felt honest. Not what promised identity. What carried quiet aliveness.

That kind of listening does not make life passive. It makes it intimate.

I still had to choose.
I still had to act.
I still had to live in time, make decisions, and shape my days.

But the source of those decisions had changed. They no longer came primarily from fear of being aimless. More and more, they came from contact with the moment itself.

That has become one of the deepest forms of relief I know. Not the relief of having it all figured out. The relief of no longer needing to.

There was a time when I thought peace would arrive as a conclusion. A final answer. A stable internal state. A clear future. A sense that I had finally gotten ahead of uncertainty. But that is not the peace I found.

The peace I found is quieter than that. It is what becomes possible when I stop demanding that life justify itself before I agree to inhabit it.

It is what appears when I stop treating uncertainty as failure.
When I stop making every open space into a problem.
When I stop asking the future to rescue me from the present.

Then ordinary life begins to look different.

A cup of coffee warming my hands in the morning.
A beam of light onto the floor.
The dog needing to go out.
The breath arriving without effort for a few unguarded seconds.
A page written with full attention.
A silence that no longer needs immediate filling.

These moments do not announce themselves as revelation. They do not look dramatic from the outside. But more and more, I have come to suspect that this is where life has been waiting all along.

Not in the future.
Not in the breakthrough.
Not in the perfected self.

Here.

In the ordinary holiness of enough.

Enoughness is not complacency. It is not giving up. It is not the denial of desire. It is the loosening of the old assumption that life is always elsewhere, always ahead, always on the other side of some improved version of me.

Enoughness says:

This moment does not need to be extraordinary in order to be real.
This day does not need to become a plan in order to matter.
This life does not need to be solved in order to be lived.

That has changed the way I understand freedom.

I once thought freedom meant certainty, mastery, or control. I thought it meant finally becoming so clear, so healed, so disciplined that I would no longer be pulled by fear, grief, anger, restlessness, or doubt.

But that is not the freedom I found. The freedom I found is smaller, humbler, and far more human. It is the freedom of participation. The freedom to notice what is happening without being entirely consumed by it. The freedom to refrain, sometimes, from obeying the first impulse. The freedom to return when I drift. The freedom to shape a response without pretending I am above conditioning.

Not mastery over life.

A more honest way of moving with it.

That honesty matters because healing did not make me less human. It did not make me less vulnerable, less uncertain, or less affected by change. It made me less afraid of being human.

I still feel old tensions rise.
I still notice the mind reaching for control.
I still feel the body lean toward urgency when life grows unclear.

The difference is not that those movements are gone. The difference is that they no longer mean the same thing.

They do not automatically mean I am lost.
They do not automatically mean I am failing.
They do not automatically mean I need to rebuild the old machinery.

Sometimes they mean only that I am alive in a nervous system with a history.
Sometimes they mean this moment is asking for gentleness.
Sometimes they mean that we begin again.

That phrase has stayed with me because it carries no demand for mastery. It does not require a perfect mind, a perfect plan, or a final answer. It asks only for return.

A return to the body.
A return to the breath.
A return to what is actually here.
A return to the next honest step.

That is enough.

Not because it solves the unknown. Because it lets me live inside it without abandoning myself.

After everything I have taken apart in these pages, this may be what remains most true for me.

Life does not always offer a map.
The reflex still rises.
The body still feels.
The old lens still colors what it sees.

But awareness can return.
The grip can soften.
The next response can be chosen.
And from that choice, a life can quietly begin again.

Not once.

Continually.

That is how I have learned to live now.

Not by outrunning uncertainty.
Not by forcing meaning.
Not by constructing a future quickly enough to calm the mind.

But by meeting what is here with enough honesty to feel it, enough awareness to notice it, and enough trust to take the next step without needing the whole path at once.

For now, that is enough.

When we stumble, when we forget, we begin again.

POSTLUDE

My hope is simple: that something in these words has helped you hear yourself more clearly. That a shift in perception might lower the volume of life's distortions just enough for your own resonance to come through.

This book began as a reckoning. A disruption. A loss I did not ask for. Beneath that rupture, something quiet waited for me, something I could not force or fix, only meet. In time, that something revealed itself as awareness. Not the kind you think your way into, but the kind that meets you where you are and walks with you as you move forward.

I used to think the point was to heal, to be done, to get it right. But there is no final draft of becoming. No fixed self to perfect. Only the practice of returning. Of noticing. Of loosening the grip long enough to meet life as it is, not as it was, and not as you fear it will be.

If this book has offered anything, I hope it has not been one more demand to improve yourself into worthiness. I hope it has offered something gentler and truer than that: a way of meeting your life with more honesty, more humility, and less fear. Not a better performance. A better relationship with what is real.

After all this writing and searching, this is what I know: a reckoning can take almost everything you thought you needed and still leave you with something truer.

Not answers.
Not certainty.
Presence.

Presence does not make life easier. It makes life real. It returns you to what is here before the mind turns it into a verdict. When you live from that place, the old game begins to loosen. You stop bargaining with reality. You stop measuring your worth against shifting conditions. You begin, little by little, to meet the world as it is, and yourself as you are.

More than a year has passed since my hearing injury. The ringing is still here, though some of the distortion has softened, offering a measure of relief. But the deeper change has not been in my ear. It has been in my capacity to listen beyond the noise, not only the noise of tinnitus, but the noise of fear, resistance, and the stories my mind once built around discomfort.

I sit here today much as I did a year ago, coffee in hand, computer resting on my lap, looking out over the same pasture. The cows still move slowly through the field. The mountains still rise beyond them, touched now by the changing light of another season. Life has continued its quiet turning.

I remember sitting in this very spot early in my reckoning and realizing, almost with surprise: In this moment, I am okay.

A year later, I am still okay.

Not healed.
Not fixed.
Not free from grief.

But okay.

That does not mean the loss has disappeared. It has not. Some part of it still lives in the fabric of my heart. But it no longer controls the way I see the world. The pain remains, but the lens has changed. I am not as easily swept into the old spin of thought, not as quickly pulled into the story that everything lost must become a verdict about the life ahead.

Something in me has adapted.

Perhaps that is growth. Perhaps it is acceptance. Perhaps it is the slow arrival of peace. What I know is this: I have learned that suffering can be met differently. I have learned that equanimity is not an idea I admire from a distance, but a habit of seeing that can be practiced, forgotten, and practiced again.

This is not resolution.

It is adaptation.

It is the quiet resilience of a human being learning to live with what remains, while remembering that even when life cannot be chosen, the way we meet it still can.

That is the hidden gift that appeared during my darkest days.

A new lens.
A new way of seeing.
A new way of responding.

If there is anything I can offer from this long season of writing, revising, grieving, resisting, and returning, it is this: the work will not stay finished.

We will forget. We will drift. The old stories will come back looking for our signature. When they do, this is not failure, just an important message.

Notice.
Soften.
Return.

Begin again.

With Deep Gratitude

This book was born from a lineage of great thinkers, teachers, and writers who shaped my understanding of suffering, awareness, and healing. It is the synthesis of many voices, some spoken in conversation, some encountered through pages, podcasts, or passing insight. Many of the ideas here were not born from my own revelations. They were gifted, lived, struggled with, and passed down by teachers who helped me see more clearly.

I do not claim to own these truths. I simply tried to live them. This is not an academic text. It's a lived reflection, an offering shaped by experience, reshaped by reckoning.

My deepest thanks go to the authors, thinkers, and fellow wanderers who made space for awareness in their own lives and, in doing so, gave me permission to begin again.

On Mindfulness and Inner Awareness

Brach, Tara. Radical Acceptance: Embracing Your Life with the Heart of a Buddha. Bantam, 2003.

Chödrön, Pema. When Things Fall Apart: Heart Advice for Difficult Times. Shambhala, 1997.

Chödrön, Pema. Welcoming the Unwelcome: Wholehearted Living in a Brokenhearted World. Shambhala, 2019.

Goldstein, Joseph. Mindfulness: A Practical Guide to Awakening. Sounds True, 2013.

Hanh, Thich Nhat. The Miracle of Mindfulness: An Introduction to the Practice of Meditation. Beacon Press, 1975.

Harris, Sam. Waking Up: A Guide to Spirituality Without Religion. Simon & Schuster, 2014.

Kabat-Zinn, Jon. Full Catastrophe Living: Using the Wisdom of Your Body and Mind to Face Stress, Pain, and Illness. Delta, 1990.

Kornfield, Jack. A Path with Heart: A Guide through the Perils and Promises of Spiritual Life. Bantam, 1993.

Salzberg, Sharon. Lovingkindness: The Revolutionary Art of Happiness. Shambhala, 1995.

Singer, Michael. The Untethered Soul: The Journey Beyond Yourself. New Harbinger, 2007.

On Trauma, Somatics, and Healing

Gendlin, Eugene. Focusing. Bantam, 1978.

Levine, Peter A. Waking the Tiger: Healing Trauma. North Atlantic Books, 1997.

Maté, Gabor. The Myth of Normal: Trauma, Illness, and Healing in a Toxic Culture. Avery, 2022.

Menakem, Resmaa. My Grandmother's Hands: Racialized Trauma and the Pathway to Mending Our Hearts and Bodies. Central Recovery Press, 2017.

Porges, Stephen W. The Polyvagal Theory: Neurophysiological Foundations of Emotions, Attachment, Communication, and Self-Regulation. Norton, 2011.

van der Kolk, Bessel. The Body Keeps the Score: Brain, Mind, and Body in the Healing of Trauma. Viking, 2014.

On Thought, Identity, and the Mind

Dweck, Carol S. Mindset: The New Psychology of Success. Random House, 2006.

Frankl, Viktor E. Man's Search for Meaning. Beacon Press, 1959.

Hollis, James. The Middle Passage: From Misery to Meaning in Midlife. Inner City Books, 1993.

Jung, C.G. Modern Man in Search of a Soul. Harcourt, Brace & World, 1933.

Kahneman, Daniel. Thinking, Fast and Slow. Farrar, Straus and Giroux, 2011.

Katie, Byron. Loving What Is: Four Questions That Can Change Your Life. Harmony, 2002.

Tolle, Eckhart. The Power of Now: A Guide to Spiritual Enlightenment. New World Library, 1999.

Merlino, Susan. The Edge of Reckoning Podcast, 2025.

To these wonderful thinkers:
You may never know the ripples of your work.

But they reached me—and helped me begin again.

Thank you.

ABOUT THE AUTHOR

Neil Freebern spent many years teaching music and technology at both the secondary and collegiate levels, while also working as a performer, composer, arranger, conductor, and music producer. These days, he spends much of his time writing, listening, and paying closer attention to his life as it unfolds.

To hear the song *Upekkhā* and explore companion materials from the writing of this book, visit soundworkproductions.com.

Directory: /Users/nfreebern/Library/Containers/com.microsoft.Word/Data
ents
Template: /Users/nfreebern/Library/Group Containers/UBF8T346G9.Offi
Content.localized/Templates.localized/Normal.dotm
Title:
Subject:
Author: python-docx
Keywords:
Comments: generated by python-docx
Creation Date: 4/29/26 1:55:00 PM
Change Number: 2
Last Saved On: 4/29/26 1:55:00 PM
Last Saved By: Neil Freebern
Total Editing Time: 1 Minute
Last Printed On: 4/29/26 1:55:00 PM
As of Last Complete Printing
Number of Pages: 99
Number of Words: 26,406
Number of Characters: 124,102 (approx.)

www.ingramcontent.com/pod-product-compliance
Ingram Content Group UK Ltd.
Pitfield, Milton Keynes, MK11 3LW, UK
UKHW021922190726
13853UKWH00002B/793